ISBN 978-0-656-05002-4
PIBN 10461803

ROYAL
AND
NOBLE AUTHORS
OF
ENGLAND,

With LISTS of their WORKS.

*Dove, diavolo! Meſſer Ludovico, avete pigliato
tante coglionerie?*

CARD. D'ESTE, to ARIOSTO.

VOL. II.

PRINTED AT STRAWBERRY-HILL.

M DCC LVIII.

NOBLE AUTHORS.

GEORGE MONKE,

DUKE of ALBEMARLE.

THIS memorable Man who raifed himfelf by his. perfonal merit within reach of a crown, which He had the prudence or the virtue to wave, whofe being able to place it on the head of the Heir is imputed to aftonifhing art or fecrecy, when in reality He only furnifhed a hand to the heart of a nation; and who after the greateft fervices that a fubject could perform, either wanted the fenfe, or had the fenfe to diftinguifh himfelf no farther; [for perhaps he was fingularly fortunate in always embracing the moment of propriety] This Man was an author; a

light

light in which He is by no means known, and
yet in which He did not want merit.   After his
death was publifhed by authority a treatife in
his own profeffion, which He compofed while
a prifoner in the tower : It is called

"Obfervations upon military and political
"affairs, written by the moft honourable George
"Duke of Albemarle, &c."   A fmall folio,
Lond. 1671.   Befides a dedication to Charles
the Second, figned John Heath, the Editor;
it contains thirty chapters of martial rules in-

reality a kind of military grammar.   Of the
fcience I am no judge :   The remarks are fhort,
fenfible and pointed.   Armour was not yet in
difufe :   He tells *his young galants* †, " That men
" wear not arms becaufe they are afraid of
" danger, but becaufe they would not fear it."
                                                            an
odd reafon for the ufe of pikes, preferably to
fwords.; " That if you arm your men with the
" latter, half the fwords amongft the common
" men will on the fyrft march be broken with
" cutting boughs ‡."

† *p.* 23.   ‡ *p.* 27.   We

We have befides

" The Speech of General Monke in the
"Houfe of Commons concerning the fettling
" the conduct of the armies of the three nations
" for the fafety thereof ‖ ."

" Speech and declaration of his Excellency
" the Lord General Monke, delivered at White-
" hall, February 21, 1659, to the Members of
" Parliament at their meeting, before the re-ad-
" miffion of the formerly fecluded Members § ."

" Letter to Gervafe Pigot † ."

" Letters written by General Monke relating
" to the Reftoration ‡ ." Lond. 1714-15.

‖ *Vide Buckingham's works, vol.* 1. *p.* 344.
§ *Somers's tracts, third coll. vol.* 2. *p.* 155.
† *Peck's Defid. curi. vol.* 1. *lib.* 6. *p.* 26.
‡ *Harl. Catal. vol.* 4. *p.* 585.

B 2   *CHARLES*

CHARLES STANLEY,

EARL of DERBY,

A Peer of whom extremely little is known. His Father loft his head, and He his liberty for Charles the Second. The grateful King rewarded the Son with the Lord-Lieutenancies of two Counties. He has written a piece of controverfy, the title of which is,

" The Proteftant religion is a fure, foundation "of a true Chriftian and a good fubject, a great " friend to human fociety, and a grand promo- " ter of all virtues, both chriftian and moral. " By Charles Earl of Derby, Lord of Man and " the Ifles." Lond. 1671, the fecond edition; a very thin quarto.

This

This piece contains a dedication " To all
" Supreme Powers, by what titles foever dig-
" nified or 'diftinguifhed, *i. e.* 'to' Emperors,
" Kings, Sovereign Princes, Republics, &c."
An Epiftle to the Reader ; another longer on the
fecond edition ; and the work itfelf, which is a
Dialogue between Orthodox, a royalift, and
Cacodæmon, one popifhly affected. His Lordfhip is warm againft the Church of Rome, their
Cafuifts, and the Jefuits ; and feems well read
in the Fathers and in polemic divinity, from
both which his ftyle has adopted much acri-
mony. He died in 1672. His Father, as has
been faid, was the brave James Earl of Derby ;
his Mother, the Heroine who defended Latham-
houfe, Grand-daughter of the Great Prince
of Orange : A compound of Proteftant Heroifm that evaporated in controverfy.

JOHN

JOHN POWLETT,

MARQ^{s.} of WINCHESTER,

GRANDSON of the Marquis mentioned above; an imitator of the Earl of Monmouth, whom I may call *the Tranflator*; like the preceding Lord, a prodigious fufferer for the royal caufe, and not more bountifully rewarded. Indeed one does not know how to believe what our hiftories record, that his houfe at Bafing, which He defended for two years together, and which the Parliamentarians burned in revenge, contained money, jewels, and furniture, to the value of two hundred thoufand pounds. Of what was compofed the bed valued at fourteen thoufand pounds? In every window the Marquis wrote with a diamond, *aimez Loyauté.* His epitaph was the compofition of Dryden.

His

His Lordship tranflated from French into Englifh

" The gallery of heroic Women." Lond. 1652.

" Talon's holy hiftory." Lond. 1653. quº.

And other books, which, fays Antony Wood, I have not yet feen *.

WILLIAM CAVENDISH,

DUKE of NEWCASTLE;

A Man extremely known from the courfe of life into which he was forced, and who would foon have been forgotten in the walk of fame which he chofe for himfelf. Yet as an author He is familiar to thofe who fcarce know any other author-------from his book of horfe-

* _vol. 2. p. 525._

manfhip,

manſhip. Though *amorous in poetry and muſic,* as my Lord Clarendon ſays *, he was fitter to break Pegaſus for a manage, than to mount him on the ſteeps of Parnaſſus. Of all the riders of that ſteed perhaps there have not been a more fantaſtic couple than his Grace and his faithful Ducheſs, who was never off her pilion. One of the noble Hiſtorian's fineſt portraits is of this Duke: The Ducheſs has left another; more diffuſe indeed, but not leſs entertaining. It is equally amuſing to hear her ſometimes compare her Lord to Julius Cæſar, and oftner to acquaint you with ſuch anecdotes, as in what ſort of coach he went to Amſterdam. The touches on her own character are inimitable; She ſays †, " That it pleaſed God to command " his ſervant Nature to *indue* her with a poetical " and philoſophical genius even from her birth, " for She did write ſome books even in that kind " before She was twelve years of age." But though She had written philoſophy, it ſeems She had read none, for at near forty She informs us

* *vol.* 2. *p.* 507.
† *Dedication.*

that

that She applied to the reading of philofophic authors------" in order to learn the terms of "art ‡." But what gives one the beft idea of her unbounded paffion for fcribling, was her feldom revifing the copies of her works, *left it ſhould diſturb her following conceptions.* What a picture of foolifh nobility was this ftately poetic couple, retired to their own little domain, and intoxicating one another with circumftantial flattery, on what was of confequence to no mortal but themfelves! In that repofitory of curious portraits at Welbeck is a whole length of the Duchefs in a theatric habit, which Tradition fays She generally wore. Befides Lord Clarendon's defcription, and his own Duchefs's life of this Nobleman, there is a full account of him in the Biographia Britannica ‖, where the ample encomiums would endure fome abatement. He feems to have been a man in whofe Character Ridicule would find more materials than Satire.

‡ *ibid.*

‖ *p.* 1214.

He publifhed

" La methode nouvelle de dreffer les chevaux;
" avec figures; or the new method of manag-
" ing horfes; with cuts." Antwerp, 1658. fol.
This was firft written in Englifh, and tranflated
into French by a Walloon.

" A new method and extraordinary invention
" to drefs horfes, and work them according to
" nature by the fubtlety of art." Lond. 1667.
folio. This fecond piece, as the Duke informs
his reader, " is neither a tranflation of the firft,
" nor an abfolute neceffary addition to it; and
" may be of ufe without the other, as the other
" hath been hitherto, and ftill is, without this.
" But both together will queftionlefs do beft."
A noble edition of this work has been printed of
late years in this kingdom.

" The Exile, a Comedy § ."

" The Country Captain, a Comedy; " written during his banifhment, and printed at Ant-

§ *Vide Theatr. records, p.* 57.

werp,

werp, 1649 : Afterwards prefented by his Majefty's fervants at Black-fryars, and very much
commended by Mr. Leigh.

"Variety, a, Comedy;" prefented by his
Majefty's fervants at Black-fryars : Firft printed
in 1649, and generally bound with the Country
Captain. 'It was alfo highly commended in a
copy of verfes by Mr. Alexander Brome.

"The Humorous Lovers, a Comedy;" acted
by his Royal Highnefs's fervants. Lond. 1677.
qu°. This was received with great applaufe,
and efteemed one of the beft plays at that
time.

"The triumphant Widow, or the medley of
"Humours, a Comedy;" acted by his Royal
Highnefs's fervants. Lond. 1677. qu°. This
piece pleafed Mr. Shadwell fo much, that He
tranfcribed part of it into his Bury-fair, one of the
moft fuccefsful plays of that Laureate. His Biographer fays, "That his Grace wrote in the
"manner of Ben Johnfon, and is allowed by

"the

" the beft judges not to have been inferior to his
" mafter." I cannot think thefe panegyrics very
advantageous: What compofitions, that imitated Johnfon's pedantry, and mixed well with
Shadwell's poverty! Johnfon, Shadwell, and
Sir William Davenant, were all patronized by
the Duke;

His poems are fcattered among thofe of his
Dutchefs, in whofe plays too he wrote many
fcenes.

One does not know whether to admire the
philofophy or fmile at the triflingnefs of this and
the laft-mentioned Peer, who after facrificing
fuch fortunes ‖ for their mafter, and during
fuch calamities of their country, could accomo-
date their minds to the utmoft idleneffes of
litterature.

‖ *It is computed by the Duchefs of Newcaftle, that
the lofs fuftained by the Duke from the civil wars,
rather furpaffed than fell fhort of £.733,579. Vide
the life.*

EDWARD

EDWARD HYDE,

EARL of CLARENDON,

F O R, his comprehenfive knowledge of Man-kind ftyled *, *The Chancellor* of *human Na-ture.* His character at this diftance of time may, ought to be impartially confidered. His defigning or blinded cotemporaries heaped the moft unjuft abufe upon him : The fubfequent age, when the partizans of prerogative were at leaft the foudeft, if not the moft numerous, fmit with a work that deified their Martyr, have been unbounded in their encomiums. We fhall fteer a middle courfe, and feperate his great virtues, which have *not* been the foundation of his fame, from his faults as an Hiftorian, the real fources of it.

---

* *Vide critical and philofophical Inquiry into the caufes of prodigies and miracles as related by hifto-rians, quoted in Gen. Dict.* vol. 6. p. 341.

Of

Of all modern virtues Patriotifm has ftood the Teft the worft. The great Strafford with the eloquence of Tully and the heroifm of Epaminondas, had none of the fteadinefs of the latter. Hampden, lefs ftained, cannot but be fufpected of covering ambitious thoughts with the mantle of popular virtue.-----In the partition of employments on a treaty with the King, his *contenting* himfelf with afking the poft of Governor to the Prince feems to me to have had at leaft as deep a tincture of felf-interestednefs, as my Lord Strafford had, who ftrode at once from Demagogue to Prime-minifter. Sir Edward Hyde, who oppofed an arbitrary court, and embraced the party of an afflicted one, muft be allowed to have acted confcientiously. A better proof was his behaviour on the Reftoration, when the torrent of an infatuated Nation entreated the King and his Minifter to be abfolute. Had Clarendon fought nothing but power, his power had never ceafed. A corrupted court and a blinded populace were lefs the caufes of the Chancellor's fall, than an ungrateful King, who could not pardon his Lordfhip's having refufed to accept for him the flavery of his country.

In

In this light my Lord Clarendon was more *the Chancellor* of *human Nature*, than from his knowledge of it. Like Justice itself he held the balance between the necessary power of the supreme Magistrate and the interests of the People. This never-dying obligation his cotemporaries were taught to overlook and to clamour against, till they removed the only Man, who, if He could, would have corrected his Master's evil government. One reads with indignation that buffooneries too low and insipid for Bartholemew-fair were practiced in a court called *polite*, to make a silly man of wit laugh himself into disgracing the only honest Minister he had. Buckingham, Shaftesbury, Lauderdale, Arlington, and such abominable Men were the exchange which the Nation made for my Lord Clarendon! It should not be forgot that Sir Edward Seymour carried up the charge against him, and that the Earl of Bristol had before attempted his ruin, by accusing him of being at once an enemy and a friend to the Papists. His Son-in-law † did not think him

† *The Duke of York.*

the

the latter, or he would have interpofed more warmly in his behalf.

Thefe I have mentioned, and almoft every virtue of a Minifter make his Character vener-able. As an Hiftorian He feems more excep-tionable. His majefty and eloquence, his power of painting characters, his knowledge of his fubject, rank him in the firft clafs of Writers----yet he has both great and little faults. Of the latter, his ftories of ghofts and omens are not to be defended by fuppofing He did not believe them himfelf: There can be no other reafon for inferting them, nor is there any medium between believing and laughing at them. Per-haps even his favorite character of Lord Falk--land takes too confiderable a fhare in the hiftory: One loves indeed the heart that believed till He made his friend the Hero of his Epic. His capital fault is, his whole work being a laboured juftification of King Charles. No Man ever delivered fo much truth with fo little fincerity. If He relates faults, fome palliating epithet al-ways flides in; and He has the art of breaking his darkeft fhades with gleams of light that take

off

off all impreſſion of horrour.-----One may-pro-
nounce on my Lord Clarendon in his double
capacity of Stateſman and Hiſtorian, that He
acted for liberty, but wrote for prerogative. .

There have been publiſhed of his Lordſhip's
writing

" Many Letters to promote the Reſtoration ‖ ."

" Several Speeches in Parliament during his
" Chancellorſhip, from the Reſtoration to
" 1667;" at leaſt ten of them.

" A full anſwer to an infamous and traiterous
" pamphlet, intituled, a Declaration of the
" Commons of England in Parliament aſſembled,
" expreſſing the grounds and reaſons of paſſing
" their late reſolutions touching no farther ad-
" dreſs or application to be made to the King."
Lond. 1648. quᵒ.

‖ Printed in vitâ Johannis Barwick. ⸸ Vide
Gen: Dict. vol. 6. p. 336; and Biogr. Britan.
vol. 4. p. 2332.

" The difference and difparity between the
" eftates and conditions of George Duke of
" Buckingham and Robert Earl of Effex.
" Printed in the Reliquiæ Wottonianæ." Lond.
1672. octavo. It is a kind of anfwer to Sir
Henry Wotton's parallel of thofe two Favorites,
and though written when Mr. Hyde was very
young, is much preferable to the affected author
it anfwers.

" Animadverfions on a book called, Fanati-
" cifm fanatically imputed to the Catholic
" Church by Dr. Stillingfleet, and the imputa-
" tion refuted and retorted by J. C. By a per-
" fon of honour." Lond. 1674. octavo. Twice
printed that year.

" A Letter to the Duke of York, and ano-
" ther to his daughter the Duchefs, on her em-
" bracing the Roman Catholic religion." I

" A brief view and furvey of the dangerous
" and pernicious errors to the Church and State,
" in Mr. Hobbes's book intituled, Leviathan."
Oxf.

Oxf. 1676. qu°. The Dedication to the King is dated at Moulins, May 10, 1673.

He made likewife alterations and additions to a book intituled,

" A collection of the orders heretofore ufed " in Chancery." Lond. 1661. octavo. His Lordfhip was affifted in this work by Sir Har- bottle Grimftone, Mafter of the Rolls.

" Hiftory of the Rebellion and civil wars in " Ireland," printed at London in folio, 1726.

" Hiftory of the Rebellion." The firft volume was printed at Oxford in folio, 1702; the fecond in 1703; the third in 1704. It has been feveral times re-printed fince in fix volumes octavo. A French tranflation was printed at the Hague in 1704 and 1709, twelves.

His Lordfhip left befides in manufcript a fe- cond part of his Hiftory; a performance long detained from, though eagerly defired by, and

at

at laſt bequeathed to the Public by his Lordſhip's amiable Deſcendent and Heir ⸱of his Integrity, the late Lord Hyde and Cornbury. Yet this important Work has not yet ſeen the Light! ‡.

GEORGE DIGBY,
EARL of BRISTOL;

A Ṣingular Perſon, whoſe life was one con-tradiction. He wrote againſt Popery and embraced it; He was a zealous oppoſer of the Court, and a ſacrifice for it: Was conſcien-tiouſly converted in the midſt of his proſecution of Lord Strafford, and was moſt unconſcien-tiouſly a Proſecutor of Lord Clarendon. With

‡ *It is not of conſequence enough to form a ſepe-rate article, and therefore I ſhall only mention here, that Henry Earl of Clarendon, eldeſt Son of the Chancellor, drew up an account of the monuments in the Cathedral at Wincheſter in* 1683, *which was continued, and was printed with the hiſtory of that Church by Roger Gale,* 1715.

great

great parts, He always hurt himſelf and his
friends; ·with romantic bravery, He was always
an unſucceſsful Commander. He ſpoke for the
Teſt-act though a Roman Catholic, and addict-
ed himſelf to Aſtrology on the birth-day of true
Philoſophy.

We have of his writing

" Letters between the Lord George Digby,
" and Sir Kenelm Digby, Knight, concerning
" Religion." Lond. 1651. This was a con-
troverſy on Popery, in which Lord Digby ſhews
that the Roman Catholic religion has no foundation on tradition, or on the authority of the
Fathers, &c. Sir Kenelm was not only a
Papiſt, but an Occult Philoſopher: If Lord
Digby had happened to laugh at that nonſenſe
too, He would probably have died in ſearch of
the Grand Elixir.

" Several Speeches*."

" Several Letters†."

* A. Wood, vol. 2. p. 579.
† ibid.   " A letter

" A Letter to Charles the Second, on being
" banifhed from his prefence ‡."

" Elvira, or the worft not always true; a
" Comedy." For this He was brought into Sir
John Suckling's Seffion of Poets.

" Excepta è diverfis operibus Patrum Lati-
" norum. M S. ‖ "

" The three firft books of Caffandra;" tranflated from the French, 8vo.

He is faid to be author of

" A true and impartial relation of the battle,
" between his Majefty's army and that of the
" Rebels near Ailefbury, Bucks, September 20,
" 1643."

And I find under his name, though probably
not of his writing, the following piece,

" Lord Digby's arcana aulica, or Walfing-
" ham's manual of prudential maxims for the
" Statefman and the Courtier, 1655 §."

‡ *Collection of letters, vol.* 2. *p.* 51.
‖ *Wood, ib.*
§ *Harl. Catal. vol.* 2. *p.* 755.   DENZIL

DENZIL LORD *HOLLES*:

A Character very unlike the Earl of Briftol's; the one embraced a party with levity, and purfued it with paffion; the other took his part on reflection, and yet could wave it, though his paffions were concerned. The Courage of Digby blazed by choice; that of Holles * burned by neceffity. Through their life, the former acted from the impulfe of great parts; the latter of common fenfe; and in both the event was what in thofe cafes, it generally is, Digby was unfortunate and admired; Holles was fuccefsful and un-renowned.

* *A remarkable inftance of his Spirit was his challenging General Ireton, who pleading "That "his Confcience would not permit him to fight a "duel," Holles, pulled him by the Nofe, telling him, "That if his Confcience would not let him "give redrefs, it ought to prevent him from offer- "ing Injuries."*

On a ftrict difquifition into the conduct of the latter, He feems to have been a Patriot both by principle and behaviour, 'and to have thoroughly underftood the ftate of his country, and it's relations with Europe, it's dangers from royal power, from ufurpation, from anarchy, from popery, from the increafe of the French empire: On every crifis I have mentioned He acted an honeft and uniform part. He early oppofed the enormous exertion of the Prerogative by Charles the Firft and his Minifters, carrying up the impeachment againft Laud, fuffering a fevere imprifonment for his free fpirit, and being marked by the King in that wild attempt of accufing the five Members. Yet He feems to have been one of the firft alarmed at the defigns of thofe who propofed to chaftife as well as to correct; and who meaned to retain the power as well as the office of punifhment. At the Treaty at Oxford where He was one of the Commiffioners from the Parliament, He ventured, in hopes of healing the diftractions, to advife the King what to anfwer, an employment that clafhed a little with his truft, and in which his fagacity did not fhine, ſhine, for though the King followed his advice, it had no effect. However, the intention ſeemed upright; and his ſo eaſily forgetting the perſonal injuries He had received, reflects great honour on his memory. He refuſed to act in the proſecution of Lord Strafford, who was his Brother-in-law, and againſt the Biſhops; yet He was eſteemed the Head of the Preſbyterian party; and in the iſle of Wight adviſed his Majeſty to give up Epiſcopacy. The defects of his character ſeem to have been, that his principles were † ariſtocratic, [demonſtrated by all experience to be the moſt tyrannous ſpecies of government, and never imbibed but by proud and ſelf-intereſted men] that his oppoſition to the Army was too much founded on a perſonal enmity to Cromwell; and that He ſat on the

† *It has been objected to me, that Lord Holles's writings ſeem to argue for Democracy; but it is certain that the tenor of his conduct and of his memoires was to oppoſe and revile the low-born and popular Leaders, as ſoon as they had deprived his Lordſhip and his Aſſociates of their aſcendant in the Common-wealth. It is in vain for a man to pretend to democratic principles, who prefers Monarchy to the conſtant, natural and neceſſary conſequences of a Democracy.*

trials

trials of the Regicides, who at worſt but chaſ-
tized the faults which his Lordſhip had pointed
out. Lord Holles acted zealouſly for the Reſtoration, and while the dawn of the King's
reign was unclouded, accepted employments and
embaſſies from the Crown, conſiſtent with his
honour and duty to his Country. As ſoon as
the Catholic rudder was uncovered, He again
reverted to patriot oppoſition. When Sir William Temple's Privy-council was eſtabliſhed,
Lord Holles, though eighty-two, yet never
thinking himſelf paſt ſerving his country, accepted a place in it; but died ſoon after.

While He was an Exile in France, he wrote

" Memoirs of Denzil Lord Holles, Baron
" of Isfield in Suſſex, from the year 1641 to
" 1648." Publiſhed in 1699. They are little
more than an apology for his own conduct, and
a virulent ſatire on his Adverſaries. The extraordinary wording of the Dedication takes off all
hopes of impartiality: It is addreſſed " To the
" unparalleled couple, Mr. Oliver St. John,
" his Majeſty's Sollicitor-general, and Mr.
" Oliver Cromwell, the Parliament's Lieute-
" nant-

"nant-general, the two grand Defigners of "the ruin of three Kingdoms." Much temper was not to be expected from an exile in a religious and civil war: From the extreme good fenfe of his Lordfhip's fpeeches and letters, one fhould not have expected that weak attempt to blaft Cromwell for a Coward. How a Judicatory in the *Temple of Fame* would laugh at fuch Witneffes ‡ as a Major-general Crawford, and a Colonel Dalbier! Cæfar and Cromwell are not amenable to a commiffion of oyer and terminer.

There are publifhed befides

" Two Letters to the Earl of Strafford ‖;" publifhed among the Strafford-papers.

" A Speech in behalf of Sir Randal Crew §," who had been Chief-juftice of the King's-bench,

‡ *Two obfcure men whom Lord Holles quotes to prove inftances of Cromwell's want of fpirit.*

‖ *Vide that Collection, and Collins's hiftorical account of the families of Cavendifh, Holles, &c. p.* 100.

§ *Printed in the diurnal Occurrencies, p.* 261; *and in Collins, p.* 111.

but

but was removed for delivering his opinion againſt Loan-money.

"Another*," very good.

"Speech in Parliament, January 31, 1642, "upon the poor Tradeſmen's petition †."

"Speech at the Lord's bar, January 15, 1642, "upon the impeachment of the Earls of Nor- "thampton, Devonſhire, Monmouth, &c ‡."

"Speech in the Guildhall ‖."

"His Speech as Chairman of the Committee "on the Reſtoration §."

"A fine Letter to Monſieur Van Benning- "hen, [who had been Embaſſador in England

* *ibid.*
† *Catalogue of the Middle Temple library, p.* 492.
‡ *ib. p.* 491.
‖ *ib. p.* 493.
§ *Commons's Journal, vol.* 10. *p.* 49.

"from

" from Holland] to promote an union againſt
" France *."

" A Letter from Paris to Sir William Morrice,
" Secretary of State †."

" His Remains," being a ſecond letter to a
friend concerning the Judicature of the Biſhops
in Parliament, 1682 ‡.

" Grand Queſtion concerning the Judicature
" of the Houſe of Peers ſtated ‖."

" A pamphlet," in vindication of ſome French
gentlemen falſely accuſed of a robbery §.

* *Printed originally in quarto, and in Collins
ubi ſupra, p.* 152.
† *ib. p.* 159.
‡ *Biogr. vol.* 4. *p.* 2651.
‖ *I have met with this title no where but in the
Harl. Catal. vol.* 4. *p.* 771.
§ *Biogr. vol.* 4. *p.* 2649.

DUDLEY

DUDLEY LORD *NORTH*,

SON of the Lord before-mentioned, was made a Knight of the Bath in .1616, at the creation of Charles Prince of Wales, and fat in many Parliaments, till fecluded by the prevailing party in that which condemned the King. From that period Lord North lived privately in the country, and as the Biographer * of the Family informs us, towards the latter end of his life entertained himfelf with juftice-bufinefs,. books, and (as a very numerous iffue required) œconomy, on which fubject, befides the enfuing.pieces, he wrote

" A little Tract."

" Paffages relating' to the long Parliament," with an apologetic, or rather recantation-preface. He had it feems at firft been active againft the King.

* *Vide Roger North's life of Lord Keeper Guildford, in the preface.*

" Hiftory

" Hiſtory of the life of the Lord Edward
" North, the firſt Baron of the Family." Addreſſed to his eldeſt Son. -Written ſenſibly and in
a very good ſtyle, yet in vain attempting to give a
favorable impreſſion of his Anceſtor, who appears to have been a very time-ſerving perſon:
Though Chancellor of the augmentation-office
on the ſuppreſſion of Convents, and though He
had married his Son to the Duke of Northumberland's Daughter-in-law, he was immediately
in favour with Queen Mary and made a Baron
by Her !

" Eſſays †." Printed in 1682. The ſubjects
are, " I. Light in the way to Paradiſe. II. Of
" Truth. III. Of Goodneſs. IV. Of Eter-
" nity. V. Of original Sin."

† *Collins's peerage, vol. 4. p. 260. laſt edit.*

JAMES

JAMES TOUCHET,
EARL of CASTLEHAVEN
AND
BARON AUDLEY.

IF this Lord, who led a very martial life, had not taken the pains to record his own actions, (which however He has done with great franknefs and ingenuity) we fhould know little of his ftory, our hiftorians fcarce mentioning him; and even our writers of anecdotes as Burnet, or of tales and circumftances as Roger North, not giving any account of a court-quarrel occafioned by his Lordfhip's Memoirs. Antony Wood alone has preferved this event, but has not made it intelligible. The Earl was a Catholic; far from a bigotted one, having 'ftifly oppofed the Pope's Nuntio in Ireland†,

---

† *Vide his Memoirs*, *p.* 121.

and

and treating the Monks with very little ceremony when He found them dabling in fedition †. He himfelf had been a commander in the Irifh rebellion for the confederate Catholics, but afterwards made all the amends He could to the King's caufe, ferving under the Marquiffes of Ormond and Clanrickarde. A little before the ruin of the latter, Lord Caftlehaven was difpatched by Him to the young King at Paris, whofe fervice when he found defperate, He engaged with the great Prince of Condè then in rebellion; attended that Hero in moft of his celebrated actions; returned to England on the Reftoration; entered into the Spanifh fervice in Flanders, was witnefs to the unfuccefsful dawn of King William's glory; and died in 1684. He wrote

"The Earl of Caftlehaven's review, or his me-
" moirs of his engagement and carriage in the
" Irifh wars." Enlarged and corrected with an appendix and poftfcript. Lond. 1684. This I fuppofe was the fecond edition. The Earl had

† *ib. p.* 142.

been much cenfured for his fhare in the Irifh rebellion and wrote thefe memoirs to explain his conduct rather than to excufe it, for he freely confeffes his faults, and imputes them to provocations from the government of that kingdom, to whofe rafhnefs and cruelty conjointly with the votes and refolutions of the English parliament, He afcribes the maffacre. There are no dates, little method, and lefs ftyle in thefe memoirs; defects atoned in fome meafure by a martial honefty. Soon after their publication the Earl of Anglefey, Lord privy-feal, wrote to afk a copy. Lord Caftlehaven fent him one, but denying the work as his. Anglefey, who had been a Commiffioner in Ireland for the Parliament, thinking himfelf affected by this narrative, publifhed Caftlehaven's letter, with obfervations and reflections very abufive on the Duke of Ormond, which occafioned, firft a printed controverfy, and then a trial before the privy-council; the event of which was, that Anglefey's firft letter was voted a fcandalous libel, and himfelf removed from the cuftody of the privy-feal; and that the Earl of Caftlehaven's memoirs on which he was feveral times examined, and which He owned, were declared a fcan-

dalous

dalous libel on the government : A cenfure that feems very little founded : There is not a word that can authorize that fentence from the council of Charles the Second; but the imputation on the Lords-juftices of Charles the Firft; for I fuppofe the privy-council did not pique themfelves on vindicating the honour of the Republican Parliament ! Bifhop Morley wrote " a true " account of the whole proceedings betwixt " James Duke of Ormond, and Arthur Earl " of Anglefey ‡." folio. More of this affair will be found in the article of Anglefey.

HENRY PIERPOINT,
MARQ.ˢ of DORCHESTER,

APPEARED but little in the character of an author, though he feems to have had as great foundation for being fo, as any on the lift. He * ftudied ten and twelve hours a

‡ *Wood, vol. 2. p.* 774.
* *Wood's Fafti, vol.* 2. *p.* 22.

day

day for many years ; was admitted a Bencher
of Gray's-Inn for his knowledge of the law,
and Fellow of the College of Phyficians for his
proficience in medicine and anatomy.

He publifhed

"A Speech, fpoken in the Houfe of Lords
"concerning the right of Bifhops to fit in Par-
"liament," May 21, 1641."

"Another, concerning the lawfulnefs and
"conveniency of their intermedling in tempo-
"ral affairs, May 24, 1641."

"Speech to the trained bands of Notting-
"hamfhire at Newark, July 13, 1642."

"Letter to John Lord Roos, February 25,
"1659." This Lord was Son-in-law to the
Marquis, and was then profecuting a divorce
from his Wife for adultery. Wood fays, that
this Lord Roos, [afterwards Duke of Rutland]
affifted by Samuel Butler, returned a buffoon
anfwer, to which the Marquis replied with another paper intituled

"The

"The reafons why the Marquis of Dor-
"chefter printed his letter, together with his
"anfwer to a printed paper called, a true and
"perfect copy of the Lord Roos his anfwer to
"the Marquis of Dorchefter's letter.

Wood adds, "He, the faid Marquis, hath
"as it is probable other things extant, or at
"leaft fit to be printed, which I have not yet
"feen."

JOHN WILMOT,

EARL of ROCHESTER;

A Man, whom the Mufes were fond to in-
fpire, and afhamed to avow, and who
practiced without the leaft referve that fecret
which can make verfes more read for their defects than for their merits: The art is neither
commendable nor difficult. Moralifts proclaim
loudly that there is no wit in indecency: It is

very

very true: Indecency is far from conferring wit; but it does not deſtroy it neither. Lord Rocheſter's poems have much more obſcenity than wit, more wit than poetry, more poetry than politeneſs. One is amazed at hearing the age of Charles the Second called polite: Becauſe the Preſbyterians and Religioniſts had affeĉted to call every thing by a Scripture-name, the new Court affeĉted to call every thing by it's own name. That Court had no pretenſions to politeneſs but by it's reſemblance to another age, which called it's own groſsneſs polite, the age of Ariſtophanes. Would a Scythian have been civilized by the Athenian ſtage, or a Hottentot by the Drawing-room of Charles the Second? The charaĉters and anecdotes being forgot, the ſtate-poems of that time are a heap of ſenſeleſs ribaldry, ſcarcely in rhime, and more ſeldom in metre. When Satyrs were brought to court, no wonder the Graces would not truſt themſelves there.

The writings of this *noble* and *beautiful Count,* as Antony Wood * calls him, [for his Lord-

* * *

* *Athen. Oxon, vol. 2. p.* 655.

ſhip's

fhip's vices were among the fruits of the Reftoration, and confequently not unlovely in that Biographer's eyes] in the order they were publifhed,
at leaft as they are ranged by that Author, were

"A Satire againft Mankind," printed in one
fheet in 'folio, June 1679. It is more than an
imitation of Boileau. 'One Griffith a Minifter
wrote againft it. We are told that Andrew
Marvel ufed to fay, "That, Rochefter, was the
"only Man in England that had the true vein
"of fatire." A very wrong judgment: In-
delicacy does not fpoil flattery more than it does
fatire.

"On Nothing, a poem." Printed on one
fide of a fheet of paper in two columns.

"Poems on feveral occafions." Antwerp,
[Lond] 1680. octavo. Among his poems are
fome by other hands, falfely imputed to him.
"The ramble in St. James's park," was claimed
by one Alexander Ratcliffe of Gray's-Inn. It
feems his Lordfhip, when dying, had ordered
all his immoral writings to be burned.------But
the

the age was not without it's Curls to preserve such treasures!

" A Letter on his death-bed to Dr. Burnet." Lond. 1680. one sheet folio.

" Valentinian, a tragedy of John Fletcher, " as it is altered by the late Earl of Rochester," and acted at the Theatre-royal in Drury-lane. Lond. 1685. quarto. There is prefixed by an anonymous hand a large preface and encomium on the Author and his writings.

" Poems, &c. on several occasions, with " Valentinian, a tragedy." Lond. 1691. octavo. To this edition are prefixed poems on the death of the Earl, &c.

Under the Earl's name are printed several pieces in " A collection of poems by several " hands, &c." Lond. 1693. octavo. As also

" A translation from Horace, in Examen " poeticum; the third part of miscellany " poems, &c. Lond. 1693 †.

† *page* 262. " A Song

" A Song in imitation of Sir John Eaton's " fong ‡ ."

And in the " Annual mifcellany for the year " 1694, being the fourth part of mifcellany " poems, &c." Lond. octavo ; are afcribed to Lord Rochefter; " A Lyric, imitated from Cor- " nelius Gallus ; Apollo's grief for having killed " Hyacinth by accident, in imitation of Ovid ; " and a Song.".

" A Lampoon on the Lord Mulgrave," faid to be in Mr. Sheldon's library, M S.

" On the fuppofed Author of a late poem in " defence of Satire, with Rochefter's anfwer." M S.

" The works of the Earls of Rochefter, Rof- " common, Dorfet, &c." Two volumes in one, Lond. 1718; without any name of Printer ‖ .

‡ ib. p. 424.
‖ *It was printed by Curl.*

" Fifty-four letters to Henry Saville and
" others §."

" Seven more to his Wife and Son †."

ANTONY
ASHLEY COOPER,
EARL of SHAFTSBURY.

AS Lord Rochester was immersed only in
the vices of that reign, his was an innocent character compared to those who were
plunged in it's crimes. A great weight of the
latter fell to the share of the Lord in question,
who had canted tyranny under Cromwell, practiced it under Charles the Second, and who difgraced the cause of liberty by being the busiest
inftrument for it; when every other party had
rejected him. It was the weakest vanity in him
to brag that Cromwell would have made him

§ *Vide Collection of letters, vol. 2. published by*
Dodfley, 1755.
† *Whartoniana, vol. 2.*　　　　　　King :

King: The beſt He could hope for was not to be believed; if true, it only proved that Cromwell took him for a fool. That He ſhould have acted in the trials of the Regicides ,was. but agreeable to his character--------or to his want of it! Let us haſten to his works: He was rather a copious writer for faction than an Author, for in no light can one imagine that He wiſhed to be remembred.

"A letter from, Sir Antony, Aſhley Cooper, " Thomas Scot, J. Berners, and J. Weaver, " Eſquires, delivered to the Lord Fleetwood, " owning their late actions in endeavouring to " ſecure the Tower of London, and expoſtulat- " ing his Lordſhip's defection from his engage- " ments unto the Parliament," printed in 1659, and mentioned in no catalogue of Lord Shaft- ſbury's works.

"The fundamental conſtitutions of Carolina." London, ſeven ſheets folio; dated March 1, 1669 †.

---

† *For the following liſt of his works, vide Wood, vol.* 2. *p.* 725.

"A ſea-

" A feafonable Speech made by Sir A. Afhley
" Cooper in the Houfe of Commons 1659,
" againft the new Peers and power of the Houfe
" of Lords ‡ ."

" Speech on Lord Treafurer Clifford taking
" his oath in the Exchequer, December, 5,
" 1672.

" Several Speeches to both Houfes at the open-
" ing of the Parliament, February 4, and 5,
" 1672."

" Speech to Serjeant Edward Thurland in
" the Exchequer-chamber, when he was made
" one of the Barons of the Exchequer, January
" 24, 1672." Re-printed in 1681; to fhow
the Author's mutability, it containing zealous
arguments for the prerogative, and a moft favorable character of the Duke of York.

" Speech on the Lord Treafurer Ofborn tak-
" ing his oath in the Exchequer, June 26, 1673."

‡ *Buckingham's works, vol. 1. p. 324.*

" Speech

" Speech to both Houſes of Parliament, Octo-
" ber, 27, 1673."

" Speech in the Houſe of Lords, October
" 20, 1675," upon the debate for appointing a
day to hear Dr. T. Shirley's caſe.

" Speech in the Houſe of Lords, March 25,
" 1679," upon occaſion of the Houſe reſolving
itſelf into a grand Committee to conſider the
State of England.

" Speech lately made by a noble Peer of the
" realm, Novemb: 1680." This was never
ſpoken, and was by order of the Lords, burnt
by the hands of the hangman. It flattered the
Scots; and was anſwered anonymouſly in a
pamphlet called, " A letter from Scotland,
" written occaſionally upon the Speech made
" by a noble Peer of this realm."

" Two ſeaſonable diſcourſes concerning this
" preſent Parliament," Oxon. [Lond.] 1675.
quarto. The firſt diſcourſe is intituled, " The
" debate

" debate or argmuents for diffolving this prefent
" Parliament, and the calling frequent and new
" Parliaments." The fecond, " A letter from a
" Parliament-Man to his Friend, concerning
" the proceedings of the Houfe of Commons
" this laft Seffion, begun October 13, 1675."
Both were anfwered in a book called, " A Pac-
" ket of Advices. Part I."

" A Letter from a Perfon of Quality to his
" Friend in the Country, 1675." qu°. Publifhed after the prorogation of Parliament in
November that year. It was written againft the
Teft; and was anfwered by Marchmont Need-
ham in his " Packet of Advices to the Men of
" Shaftfbury." *It is remarkable that this Need-
ham had been retained by the Regicides to write
againft the Royal Family; and was now hired by
the Court to write againft one who had been almoft
as deeply engaged againft the King.*

" His Cafe at the King's-bench on his con-
" finement in the Tower." Lond. 1679.

" Expedient

" Expedient for fettling the Nation, difcourf-
" ed with his Majefty in the Houfe of Peers at
" Oxford, March 24, 1680." Lond. 1681;
one fheet quarto. The expedient was the fettlement of the Crown on the Duke of Monmouth.

" No proteftant Plot, or the prefent pretend-
" ed confpiracy of Proteftants againft the King's
" government, difcovered to be a confpiracy of
" the Papifts againft the King and his protef-
" tant Subjects." Lond. 1681. Of this,
Lord Shaftfbury was not the avowed but re-
puted Author. His fervant, who carried it to
the prefs, is faid to have been committed to
prifon. Being partly anfwered in a pamphlet
intituled, " A plea for fucceffion in oppofition
" to popular exclufion," there was publifhed

" The fecond part of no Proteftant plot,"
Lond. 1682.

" A third part," faid to be written by one
Robert Fergufon under the direction of Shaftsbury:

bury. All the three parts were a vindication of him. The laſt was anſwered under the title of "A letter to a friend, containing certain ob- "ſervations upon ſome paſſages in a late libel "intituled, a third part, &c."

" A modeſt account of the preſent poſture of "affairs in England, with a particular reference "to the Earl of Shaftſbury's caſe; and a vin- "dication of him from two pretended letters of "a noble Peer." [Marquis of Halifax]. This was not owned. but was imputed to the Earl by Sir Roger L'Eſtrange in his Obſervator, a gazette of the oppoſite faction.

" The Earl of Eſſex's ſpeech at the delivery "of the petition to the King, January 25, "1680." The petition was for a Parliament.

Wood imputes to Shaftſbury too

"A vindication of the Aſſociation;" but at the ſame time ſays, that the Earl's ſervant being ſeized as He was carrying it to the preſs, owned it to be Ferguſon's. The ſame Author mentions the Earl's publiſhing an apology in Holland, but does not give the title of it.

" Three

" Three letters * written during his imprifon-
" ment in the Tower, to the King, to the Duke
" of York, and to a Lord, not named.".

" The Character of the Honourable William
" Haftings of Woodlands in Hampſhire, ſe-
" cond Son of Francis Earl of Huntingdon,"
printed originally in Peck's Deſiderata curioſa,
and lately in the Conoiſſeur, vol. 3. It is a curious, and well-drawn portrait of our, ancient
Engliſh gentry.

Wood ſays that among his Lordſhip's papers
were found, but uncertain if written by Him,

" Some obſervations † concerning the regulat-
" ing elections for parliament."

One cannot but obſerve with concern what
I have before remarked, that writing the life
of a Man is too apt to inſtill partiality for the
ſubject. The Hiſtory of Lord Shaftſbury in the

___

* Printed in Collins's peerage; vide Shaftſbury.
† They are printed among Somers's tracts, vol. 1.

Biographia is almoft a panegyric; whereas a bon-mot of the Earl himfelf was his trueft character: Charles the Second faid to Him one day, " Shaftfbury, 'I believe Thou art the " wickedeft fellow in my dominions." He bowed, and replied, " Of a Subject, Sir, I " believe I am."‡.

HENEAGE FINCH,

EARL of NOTTINGHAM.

FEW families have produced fo many confiderable men as the Houfe of Finch has in late reigns: Men, who have owed their preferments to themfelves, not to favour. The Lord in queftion rofe through the great fteps of the Law, from Sollicitor to Attorney-general, to Lord Keeper, to Lord Chancellor, to an Earldom. Though employed in the moft difficult part of the reign of Charles the Second,

‡ *North's examen.*

his

his character remained untainted. Antony Wood represents him as a great Temporizer. He certainly, neither offended the Court, nor the Patriots. Had he shown great partiality to the latter, there is no doubt but the King would have difmiffed Him, being by no means so dangerous a man as his predeceffor Shaftfbury. That his complaifance for the prerogative was not unbounded, was manifeft by the King being obliged to fet the feal himfelf to the Earl of Danby's pardon. The truth is, the Earl of Nottingham was neither violent nor timid. When He pronounced fentence on the Lord Vifcount Stafford, he did not fcruple to fay, "Who can doubt now that London was burned " by the Papifts?" Burnet calls this declaration indecent: If it was fo to the unhappy Convict, it was certainly no flattery to the predominant faction at court. This fpeech was reckoned the mafter-piece of his eloquence; and his eloquence was much celebrated. Burnet fays * it was affected, laboured, and too conftant on all occafions; and that his Lordfhip lived to find it much defpifed. The Bifhop allows his probity; and in

* *vol.* i. *p.* 365.

another

another place † fpeaks of him with the greateft encomiums." Dryden has drawn a beautiful character of him in his Abfalom and Achitophel under
the name of Amri. Others ‡ have called him
the Englifh Cicero, the *Englifh Rofcius.*

Pieces of his publifhed are

" Several fpeeches and difcourfes on the trials
" of the Regicides." He was then Sollicitor-
general.

" Speeches to both Houfes of Parliament,"
while Lord Keeper and Lord Chancellor.

" Speech at pronouncing fentence on William
" Lord Vifcount Stafford, December 7, 1680,"
Printed with the trial.

" Speech againft the bill of exclufion ‖."

† *Preface to the fecond volume of his Hiftory of
the Reformation.*
‡ *Wood, vol. 2. p.* 719; *where fee the following
account of his works.*
‖ *Vide Buckingham's works, vol.* 2.

" Anfwers

" Anfwers by his Majefty's command to feve-
" ral addreffes prefented to his Majefty at Hamp-
" ton-court, May 19, 1681." Lond. one
fheet folio.

" His arguments upon a decree in a caufe in
" the Howard family; wherein the feveral ways
" and methods of limiting a truft for a term of
" ten years are fully debated." Lond. 1685;
nine fheets folio.

His Lordfhip left in manufcript

" Chancery Reports."

Sir *GEORGE BOOTH,*

LORD DELAMER,

RECORDED for his activity and zeal
for the Reftoration of Charles the Second,
in whofe behalf he feized Chefter, but was de-
feated by Lambert and imprifoned in the Tower.
We

We have already remarked some instances of the scanty liberality with which that Prince rewarded some of the greatest Sufferers in his and his Father's cause. With the same impartiality we must observe how unjustly the Author of the Peerage produces Sir George Booth as an instance of ill-paid services. By some patents and letters quoted in the same place, it is plain that Sir George was a convert of the latest date; yet He had a recompence of ten thousand pounds, * a liberty of recommending six Gentlemen to the honour of Knighthood, and two for the dignity of Baronet, and was himself created a Peer. If this was flight payment, three kingdoms would not have sufficed to discharge the Monarch's and the Martyr's arrears.

His Lordship's writings were published under this title

" The works of Lord Delamer †, containing " his Lordship's speeches in Parliament, with

---

* *It is honorable both to the King and Sir George, that £. 20,000, was designed for him, but he himself desired the House of Commons to confine the grant to £. 10,000.*

† *Harl. Catal. vol.* I. *p.* 465.　　　" dis-

" difcourfes on the affairs of State." 1691. He
is faid ‡ to have left befides in manufcript, three
books in quarto, containing collections from
Scripture difpofed methodically, "*for confirming*
"*his* judgment in the doctrine of the Gofpel,
" or encouragement of his heart in the practice
" of repentance, faith, *&c.*" To which are
added fome paffages to juftify the Church of
England againft Popifh and Prefbyterian objections.

As I have not been able to meet with this
edition of Lord Delamer's works, I muft hint
to the Reader, that I am not quite certain whether the author I quote has not made a miftake,
having perhaps confounded this Lord with his
Son, of whom an account will be given in the
courfe of this work.

‡ *Vide Memorials and Characters of eminent and
worthy Perfons,* 1741. *fol. p.* 427.

LORD

LORD KEEPER

GUILDFORD,

W AS younger Son of the Lord North before-mentioned. Burnet and Kennet have given no very favorable character of the Keeper: His relation Roger North has defended him in a very bulky work, which however does not contribute much to raise our ideas either of the Writer or his Subject *. If that performance and it's companion the Examen, had nothing elfe ridiculous in them, it would be sufficient to blast their reputation, that they aim at de-

---

* It is remarkable that two Peers of this race have suffered by apologies written for them by two of their own relations; but with this difference naturally attending the performances of a sensible man and a weak one: Dudley Lord North has shown himself an artful and elegant historian; Roger North, a miserable Biographer.

crying

crying that excellent Magiſtrate the Lord Cheif-
juſtice Hale, and that Charle's the Second, and
that wretch the Duke of Lauderdale, the King's
taking money from France and the ſeizure of
the Charter of London, are ſome of the Men
and ſome of the meaſures the Author defends!

This Lord Guildford wrote

"An alphabetical Index of verbs neuter,"
printed with Lilly's grammar :· Compiled while
he was at Bury-ſchool †.

"Argument in a caſe between Soams and
"Bernadiſton ‡."

"His argument on a trial between Charles
"Howard and the Duke of Norfolk ;" printed
with that caſe.

"The King's declaration on the Popiſh plot;"
compoſed cheifly by his Lordſhip §."

† *Vide life*, *p.* 12.
‡ *ib. p.* 159.
§ *ib. p.* 259.

"A paper

" A paper on the gravitation of fluids, con-
" fidered in the bladders of fifhes *."

" An anfwer to a paper of Sir Samuel More-
" land on his ftatic barometer." This was never
printed †.

" A philofophical effay on Mufic;" printed
by Martin, printer to the Royal Society, 1677.

" Lord Cheif-juftice North's narrative to the
" Houfe of Commons, of what Bedloe had
" fworn before him at Briftol."

" A narrative of fome paffages in or relating
" to the long Parliament, by Sir Francis North,
" afterwards Lord Keeper of the great feal ‡."

" Many notes of cafes, fragments of tranf-
" actions at court," and other papers publifhed
whole or in part, in various parts of his life by
Roger North, and in the Examen.

---

* *Printed in the Philofophical Tranfactions,*
vol. 2. p. 845.
† *Life, p. 293.*
‡ *Somers's tracts, vol. 1.*

JOHN

JOHN ROBARTES,

EARL of RADNOR,

"WAS a man of a morose and cynical
"temper, juft in his adminiftration,
"but vicious under the appearances of virtue:
"Learned beyond any man of his quality,
"but intractable, ftiff and obftinate, proud and
"jealous." Thefe are Burnet's words *. Wood
fays †, He was a Colonel for the Parliament,
that He fought defperately at Edgehill, and
afterwards at Newberry, where He was Field-
marfhal, but grew to diflike the violences of
his party, and retired till the Reftoration, when
He was made Lord privy-feal, " but giving not
"that content was expected, He was fent into

* vol. 1. p. 98.
† vol. 2. p. 778.

I 2 " Ireland

" Ireland to be Lord-Lieutenant there; and
" his government being difliked, He was re-
" called and made Lord Prefident." We are
not told how He difappointed the King's expec-
tations; probably *not* by too great complaifance;
nor why his adminiftration, which Burnet calls
juft, was difliked. If it is true, that He was a
good Governor, the prefumption will be, that
his rule was not difliked by thofe to whom, but
from whom He was fent. However, not to
judge too hardly of Charles the Second, we may
not depend too much upon the Bifhop's account
of the Earl's government, if the fruits of it
were no better than thofe of his great Learning;
all that is recorded of his writing bearing this
canting title

" A difcourfe of the vanity of the creature,
" grounded on Eccles. i, 2." Lond. 1673.
octavo.

Wood fays that He left one or two more
treatifes fitted for the prefs.

ARTHUR

ARTHUR ANNESLEY,

EARL of ANGLESEY,

WHILE a private young man was engaged on the side of Charles the First, whose party he quitted early to embrace that of the Parliament : By them He was entrusted as Commissioner of Ulster, where He performed good service to the Protestant cause. Wood says he took both the Covenant and Engagement, but the latter is contradicted *. It is certain that He seems to have lain by during the reign of Cromwell, and that He was not trusted either by the Rump or the Army. When the secluded Members were restored, He returned to Parliament, and was chosen President of the Council of State, in which capacity He was active for the Restoration, and was distinguished amongst

* *Vide his life in the Biograph. Brit.*

thofe

thofe who *coming in at the eleventh hour* received greater wages than Men who had loft their all in defending the Vineyard. He was made a Baron, an Earl, Treafurer of the Navy, Commiffioner for re-fettling Ireland, Lord privy-feal, and might, we are told†, have been Prime-Minifter, if He had not declined it to avoid envy. As He declined no other power under no kind of government, this anecdote is fufpicious; and I fhould much queftion whether ever any man declined the Prime-minifterfhip for *that* reafon. Engaging in a controverfy with the Earl of Caftlehaven, as has been mentioned; and that drawing on another with the Duke of Ormond, He was difgraced; though the author of his life in the Biographia afcribes the caufe of his fall to a remonftrance which He had prefented to the King, in which He took much liberty with his Majefty, and greater with the religion of the Duke of York. This piece being refented, though it was not thought proper, fays the Biographer, to exprefs fo much, the Duke of Ormond was perfuaded to exhibit a charge

† *Happy future ftate of England, p.* 5.

againft

againſt the Earl, which was made the pretence for removing him; but for this ſecret hiſtory no authority is quoted. The Duke's letter, taxing the Earl with breach of Friendſhip, is pre-ſerved‡, is written with great ſpirit, and ſhas this remarkable period; "I was not willing " to believe that book to be of your Lordſhip's " compoſing, and hoped ſome of the ſuborned " libellers of the age had endeavoured to imitate " your Lordſhip, and not you them." The Earl's anſwer, though inferior, does not want firmnéſs. He paſſed the reſt of his time in re-tirement, and died juſt as ſome thought He would have been appointed Lord Chancellor to James the Second, in 1686. A ſuppoſition moſt improbable: I do not think ſo ill of this Lord as to believe He could ſupplant Jefferies, who was then in poſſeſſion of the Seals, and who, without derogation from the ſubſervience of any Judge that ever was, excelled in moulding the law to the purpoſes of a court.

Of this Lord we have three characters by very different hands. Antony Wood, the high-

‡ *Life ubi ſupra.*

church fatirift, reprefents him as an artful time-
ferver; by principle a Calvinift; by policy a fa-
vourer of the Papifts. Bifhop Burnet, as un-
gentle on the other fide, paints him as a tedious
and ungraceful orator, as a grave, abandoned and
corrupt man, whom no party would truft. The
benign author of the Biographia Britannica [a
work, which notwithftanding it's fingular merit
I cannot help calling Vindicatio Britannica, or a
‖ defence of every body] humanely applies his
foftening pencil, is fuccefsful in blotting out
fome § fpots, and attempts to varnifh every one.
Wood had feverely animadverted on the Earl's
fitting in Judgment on the Regicides: The Biographer extolls it as an act of the greateft loyalty
and honour: But under favour it not only appears a fervile complaifance, but glaring injuftice.
The Earl had gone moft lengths with thofe
Men; in fhort, had acted with them in open
rebellion to his Sovereign: The putting to death

‖ See particularly the lives of Dudley, affociate
of Empfon; of the Duke of Northumberland; of
Shaftfbury; and of Arlington.

§ As his not taking the engagement; and the
accufation of corruption.

that

that Sovereign could by no means be the guilty part of their oppofition. If a King, deferves to be oppofed by force of arms, He deferves death: If He reduces his fubjects to that extremity, the blood fpilt in the quarrel lies on him———the executing him afterwards is a meer formality.

That his Lordfhip failed with the times, remains notorious: Thofe principles muft be of an * accomodating temper, which could fuffer the fame Man to be Prefident of a republican council of State, and recommend him for Chancellor, to an arbitary and popifh King. Once when the Earl of Effex charged him in the Houfe of Lords with being prayed for by the Papifts; Anglefey faid, " He believed it " was not fo; but if Jews in their Synagogues, " or Turks in their Mofques would pray for " him unafked, He fhould be glad to be the " better for their devotion." Had He really been nominated to the Chancellorfhip by James the Second, probably he would have pleaded,

---

* *He was twice Commiffioner for fettling Ireland, once under the Parliament, the other time under Charles the Second.*

That it was not of his feeking, but owing to the prayers of the Catholics, and he was glad to be the better for them.

In anfwer to the Bifhop's accufation of no party trufting him, the Biographer pleads that his Lordfhip enjoyed for two and twenty years the 'confidence 'of 'Charles 'the Second. The fact † does not appear to be true; and were it true, would be no juftification : It is well known what qualifications could recommend a man to the confidence of Charles. When Lord Clarendon loft it in feven years by his merit, it were ignominy to have preferved it two and twenty.

This Earl of Anglefey wrote

"A Letter to William Lenthall, Speaker
"to the Rump, from Mr. Annefley, expoftu-
"lating with him on account of his being ex-

† *The office of Lord Privy-feal is no place of confidence, nor is it any where faid that the Earl had any particular fhare of the King's favour.*

"cluded

" cluded the Houſe for not taking the engage-
" ment;" printed in a pamphlet called " Eng-
" land's confuſion §."

" The Truth unveiled, in behalf of the
" Church of England ‡, &c." Being a vindication of Mr. John Standiſh's ſermon before the
King, 1676. This being an anſwer to Mr.
Robert Grove's vindication of the conforming
Clergy from the unjuſt aſperſion of hereſy, was
replied to by Grove; and by a letter to the
author of the vindication of Mr. Standiſh's ſermon. With *Truth unveiled* was publiſhed a
piece on Tranſubſtantiation, intituled

" Reflections on that diſcourſe, which a
" Maſter of Arts [once] of the Univerſity of
" Cambridge calls *rational*, preſented in print to
" a perſon of honour, 1676."

This was anſwered in a tract called, " Roman
" Tradition examined."

§ *Biogr. p.* 151.
‡ *Athenæ, vol.* 2. *p.* 790.

" A letter

"A letter from a person of honour in the
"country, written to the Earl of Caſtlehaven,
"being obſervations and reflections on his
"Lordſhip's memoirs concerning the wars of
"Ireland." Lond. 1681. octavo. Beſides this
letter, which occaſioned the diſpute before-mentioned, was another book publiſhed, intituled,
"Brief reflections on the Earl of Caſtlehaven's
"memoirs, written by Dr. Edmund Borlaſe,
"author of the hiſtory of the Iriſh rebellion."

"A true account of the whole proceedings
"between James Duke of Ormond, and Ar-
"thur Earl of Angleſey, before the King and
"Council, &c." Lond. 1682. fol.

"A letter in anſwer to the Duke of Or-
"mond's §."

"A letter of remarks upon Jovian." Lond.
1683,

§ *Biogr.* p. 154.

"The

"The account of Arthur Earl of Anglesey, "Lord privy-seal to your most excellent Majesty, of the true state of your Majesty's government and kingdoms, April 27, 1682." This was preserved in the collection of papers belonging to Lord Somers, and was the remonstrance hinted at above; but I do not know that it was ever printed.

"The history of the late commotions and "troubles in Ireland, from the rebellion in 1641, "till the restoration in 1660." This history is lost, and is suspected to have been purposely destroyed by persons who were interested to suppress it‡.

"The King's right of indulgence in spiritual "matters, with the equity thereof asserted." Printed by *Hen. Care*, in 1687. Of this piece, [which was calculated to attack the test and penal laws against Papists] it is remarkable, that the noble *Author* had been a republican, and passed

‡ *Collins's peerage in Anglesey.*

for

for a Prefbyterian; and that the *Printer* was the fame perfon, who in the foregoing reign had been profecuted for publifhing *The Weekly pacquet of advice from Rome*; one of the political pieces that raifed moft clamour againft the Papifts ‖.

"Memoirs, intermixed with moral, political and hiftorical obfervations, by way of difcourfe in a letter [to Sir Peter Pett] to which is prefixed a letter written by his Lordfhip during his retirement from Court in the year 1683." Lond. 1693. octavo. Publifhed by Sir Peter Pett, Knight, Advocate-general for the kingdom of Ireland, and author of "The happy future ftate of England." The title, *Memoirs*, has no kind of relation to the work, which is a fort of rambling effay, attempting at once to defend a popifh King and the Proteftant religion. The genuinenefs of thefe memoirs was difputed by his Son-in-law Lord Haverfham §.

‖ *Ant. Wood.*
§ *See the next article.*

"The

" The Earl of Anglefey's ftate of the govern-
" ment and kingdom, prepared and intended
" for his Majefty King Charles the Second, in
" the year 1682 ; but the ftorm impending
" growing fo high prevented it then. . With a
" fhort vindication of his Lordfhip from feveral
" afperfions caft on him, in a pretended letter
" that carries the title of his Memoirs." By
Sir John Thompfon, Bart. afterwards Lord
Haverfham *.

" The privileges of the Houfe of Lords and
" Commons argued and ftated in two conferen-
" ces between both Houfes, April 19, and 22,
" 1671. To which is added a difcourfe where-
" in the rights of the Houfe of Lords are truly
" afferted. With learned remarks on the feem-
" ing arguments and pretended precedents,
" offerred at that time againft their Lordfhips."
Written by the right honorable Arthur Earl of
of Anglefey, Lord privy-feal. Thefe conferences were managed by the Earl, and concern-

* Somers's traffts, vol. 1. p. 186.

ed a bill for impofitions on merchandize, which had occafioned a difpute between the two Houfes on the old fubject of the fole right of taxing, claimed by the Commons.

Befides thefe, we are † told that fome valuable pieces of this Earl have been loft, and that He wrote a certain large and learned difcourfe on the errors of Popery in his younger years, which fome of his friends would have perfuaded him to publifh at the time of the Popifh plot; but he was diffuaded by his friend Sir Peter------ probably he would not the lefs have written his piece againft the Teft.

His Diary ‡ is faid to have been in the poffef-fion of one Mr. Ryley, in 1693.

† *North's life,* p. 30.
‡ *Biogr.* p. 157. *marg. note.*

GEORGE

GEORGE VILLIERS,

DUKE of BUCKINGHAM.

WHEN this extraordinary Man, with the figure and genius of Alcibiades, could equally charm the prefbyterian Fairfax, and the diffolute Charles; when He alike ridiculed that witty King and his folemn Chancellor; when He plotted the ruin of his country with a *Cabal* of bad Minifters; or equally unprincipled fupported it's caufe with bad Patriots; one laments that fuch parts fhould have been devoid of every virtue. But when Alcibiades turns Chymift, when He is a real bubble, and a vifionary Mifer; when ambition is but a frolic; when the worft defigns are for the foolifheft ends; contempt extinguifhes all reflections on his character.

The portrait of this Duke has been drawn by four masterly hands: Burnet has hewn it out with his rough chiffel; Count Hamilton * touched it with that flight delicacy, that finishes while it seems but to sketch: Dryden † catched the living likeness; Pope ‖ compleated the historical resemblance. Yet the abilities of this Lord appear in no instance more amazing, than that being exposed by two of the greatest poets, He has exposed one of them ten times more severely. Zimri is an admirable portrait; but Bayes an original creation. Dryden satirized Buckingham; but Villiers made Dryden satirize himself.

An instance of astonishing quickness is related of this Duke: Being present at the first representation of one of Dryden's pieces of heroic nonsense, where a Lover says,

* *Vide Memoires de Grammont.*
† *Zimri in Absalom and Achitophel.*
‖ *In the epistle to Lord Bathurst.*

" My

" My wound is great, becaufe it is fo fmall."

The Duke cried out,

" Then 'twou'd be greater, were it none at all."

The play was inftantly damned.

His Grace wrote.

" The Rehearfal," 1671.

" The Chances, a comedy," altered from Fletcher.

" Reflections upon Abfalom and Achito-
" phel ‡."

" A Speech in the Houfe of Lords, Novem-
" ber, 16, 1675, for leave to bring in a bill
" of indulgence to all Proteftant Diffenters;"
printed with Lord Shaftfbury's fpeech [above-
mentioned] for appointing a day to hear Dr.
Shirley's cafe ‖.

‡ *Athenæ, vol.* 2. *p.* 806.
‖ *ib.* 725.

" A fhort

" A fhort difcourfe upon the reafonablenefs
" of men's having a religion or worfhip of God."
Lond. 1685. It paffed through three editions.
Soon after the firft edition, came out; " A fhort
" anfwer to his Grace the Duke Buckingham's
" paper concerning religion, toleration, and
" liberty of confcience ;", to which the Duke
made a ludicrous and very good anfwer,
called,

" The Duke of Buckingham his Grace's
" letter to the unknown author of a paper in-
" tituled, a fhort anfwer †, &c." Lond. 1685.
This occafioned feveral more pamphlets.

" A demonftration of the Deity," publifhed
a little before his Grace's death.

" Verfes on two lines of Mr. Edward How-
" ard ;" printed in the third part of mifcellany
poems, 1693.

† *Somers's tracts, vol. 1. p. 367.*

" A tran-

"A translation of Horace's ode beginning,
"Fortuna fævo·" In the fourth part.

"A letter to Sir Thomas Ofborn."

Befides the above, a few pieces by this Duke
are fcattered through two volumes, called

"The works of his Grace George Villiers
"late Duke of Buckingham." Lond. 1715.
Thefe volumes are a bookfeller's mifcellany,
containing various poems and fpeeches of all
times; what belong to his Grace are [in the
firft volume]

"The Reftoration, or right will take place,
"a tragi-comedy.

"The battle of Sedgmoor, a fatirical and
"political farce.

"The militant couple, or the hufband may
"thank himfelf. A fragment.

"Pindaric

" Pindaric on the death of Lord Fairfax.

" To his Miftrefs.

" A defcription of Fortune.

" Epitaph on Felton," who murdered his Grace's father. The editor pretends that this could not be written by the Duke, but I know no principles he had to prevent his being the Author. Indeed it is more bombaft than offenfive.

" A confolatory epiftle to Captain Julian, &c.

" A character of an ugly woman, or a hue " and cry after beauty," in profe, written in 1678.

" The loft Miftrefs, a complaint againft the " Countefs of * * * * * *," 1675.

This was probably the Countefs of Shrewfbury, whofe Lord he killed in a duel on her account, and who is faid to have held the Duke's horfe, difguifed like a page, during the combat; to reward his prowefs in which, She went to bed

to

to him in the fhirt ftained with her hufband's blood. The Loves of this tender pair are recorded by Pope,

Gallant and gay in Cliefden's high alcove,
The feat of wanton Shrewfbury and Love.

" Four poems by the Duke and Lord Rochefter; " Upon Nothing; a Seffion of the Poets; " a fatire on the follies of the men of the age; " and Timon, a fatire on fome new plays."

" Three letters to Lord Arlington and Lord " Berkeley."

" His examination by the Houfe of Commons, " in which he confeffed fome part of his own " bad adminiftration, and betrayed more of his " affociate Arlington."

" Speech in the Houfe of Lords, November " 16." Vide above, p. 75.

" Speech at a conference, 1675.

" Speech

" " Speech in the Houſe of Lords to prove the
" Parliament diſſolved:" For this Speech He
with Shaftſbury, Saliſbury, and the real Whig,
Wharton, were ſent to the Tower.

In the ſecond volume,

" A key to the Rehearſal.

" An account of a conference between the
" Duke and Father Fitzgerald, whom King
" James ſent to convert his Grace in his ſick-
" neſs." This has humour.

" Eſſay upon reaſon and religion," in a letter
to Nevill Pain, Eſq;

" On human reaſon," addreſſed to Matthew
Clifford, Eſq;

" Five letters, on election-affairs, &c.

" Ten little burleſque and ſatirical poems."

HENEAGE

HENEAGE FINCH,

EARL of WINCHELSEA,

FIRST Coufin of the Chancellor Nottingham, made a figure at the fame period.
He was intimate with Monke, and concerned
in the Reftoration; foon after which He was
fent Embaffador to Mahomet the Fourth.
Monke had given the Earl the government of
Dover-caftle, which was continued to him;
and when King James was ftopped at Fever-
fham, He fent for the Earl of Winchelfea, who
prevailed on the King to return to London. The
Earl voted for giving the crown to King William,
by whom he was continued Lord Lieutenant
of Kent. He died foon after in 1689. On
his return from Conftantinople, vifiting Sicily,
he was witnefs to a terrible convulfion of mount
Ætna, an account of which he fent to the

King, and which was soon after publifhed. by authority in a very thin-quarto, with this title,

   " A true and exact relation of the late pro-
" digious earthquake and eruption of mount
" Etna, or monte Gibello, &c. together with
" a more particular narrative of the fame, as it
" is collected out of feveral relations fent from
" Catania, 1669.   With a view of the moun-
" tain and conflagration."

EDWARD MONTAGU,

EARL of SANDWICH;

A Well known character in our hiftory, and one of the moft beautiful in any hiftory. He fhone from the age of nineteen, and united the qualifications of General, Admiral, and Statefman. ...All parties, at a time when there was nothing but parties, have agreed that his virtues were equal to his valour and abilities.

His

His few blemishes are not mentioned here, but as a proof 'that' this elogium' is not a' phantom of the imagination. His advising the Dutch war was a fatal error to himself, and might have been so to his country and to the liberty of Europe. 'His persuading Cromwell to take the Crown was an unaccountable infatuation, especially as his Lordship was so zealous afterwards for the Restoration. It seems he had a fond and inexplicable passion for Royalty, though He had early acted against Charles the First. The Earl admired Cromwell; yet could He imagine that in any light a diadem would raise the Protector's character? Or how could a Man who thought Cromwell deserved a Crown, think that Charles the Second deserved one? If his Lordship supposed English minds so framed to Monarchy that they must recoil to it, was Cromwell a Man to be tender of a Constitution, which Charles the First had handled too roughly?* The Earl's zeal for restoring Charles

the

---

* It is often urged with great emphasis, that when a nation has been accustomed for ages to some particular form of government, it will [though that form of government may be changed for a time]

the Second could not flow from any principle of hereditary right, for He had contributed to dethrone the Father, and had offerred the Son's crown to the Ufurper. Lord Sandwich was facrificed by another Man having as weak a partiality for royal blood: His Vice-admiral, Sir Jofeph Jordan, thought the Duke of York's life better worth preferving, and abandoned the Earl to the Dutch firefhips!

It is remarkable that Admiral Montagu was the laft Commoner who was honoured with the Garter, except one Man, to whofe virtues and merit may fome impartial pen do as much juftice, as I have a fatisfaction in rendering to this great Perfon!

time] *always revert to it. No argument feems to me to have lefs folidity; for unlefs the climate, the air, and the foil of a country can imbibe habits of government or infufe them, no Country can in reality have been accuftomed to any fort of government, but during the lives of it's actual inhabitants. Were Men, born late in the reign of Charles the Firft, bred to entertain irradicable prejudices in favour of royalty? It is fuppofed that no country is fo naturally propenfe to liberty, as England.---- Is it naturally propenfe to Monarchy too?----Is Monarchy the natural vehicle of liberty?*

We

We have of his Lordſhip's writing,

" A letter to Secretary Thurloe †."

" Several letters during his embaſſy to Spain;" publiſhed with Arlington's letters. ' A great character of ' theſe diſpatches ' is ' given in the lives of the Admirals ‡.

" Original letters and negotiations of Sir
" Richard Fanſhaw, the Earl of Sandwich, the
" Earl of Sunderland, and Sir William Go-
" dolphin, wherein divers matters between the
" three Crowns of England, Spain and Portu-
" gal, from the year 1663, to 1678, are ſet in
" a clear light." Two vols.

And a ſingular tranſlation, called,

" The art of metals, in which is declared
" the manner of their generation, and the con-
" comitants of them. In two books. Written
" in Spaniſh by Albaro Alonzo Barbi, M. A.

† *Vide Thurloe's ſtate-papers, vol. 1. p. 726.*
‡ *vol. 2. p. 402.*

" curate

" curate of, St. Bernard's parifh in the imperial
" city of Potofi in the kingdom of Peru in the
" Weft-Indies, in the year 1640. Tranflated
" in the year 1669, by the right honourable
" Edward Earl of Sandwich."   Lond. 1674.
a fmall octavo.   A fhort preface of the Editor
fays, " The original was regarded in Spain and
" the Weft-Indies as an ineftimable jewel, but
" that falling into the Earl's hands, he enriched
" our language with it, *being content that all our*
" *Lord the King's people fhould be philofophers.*"

GEORGE SAVILLE,

MARQUIS of HALIFAX,

A Mani more remarkable for his wit than
his fteadinefs, and whom an ingenious
modern * Hiftorian has erected into a principal

---

* *Mr. Hume; who obferves that the Marquis's
variations might be the effects of his integrity,
rather than of his ambition. They might; but it
is doubtful.*

character

character in the reign of Charles the Second. But when old histories, are re-written, it is necessary to set, persons and facts in new lights from what they were seen by cotemporaries †. Voltaire, speaking of Dupleix, says ‡, that he was the first who introduced the custom of quoting his authorities in the margin, "precaution "absolument necessaire, quand on n'ecrit pas "l'histoire de son tems." However, the Dictator of this sentence, and author of that beautiful essay on Universal History, has totally forgot his own rule, and has indeed left that work a most charming bird's-eye landscape, where one views the whole in picturesque confusion, and imagines the objects more delightful than they are in reality, and when examined seperately. The Marquis wrote

" The anatomy of an equivalent ∥."

† *In order to which it is best to omit referring even to those authors that are used in the compilation.*
‡ *Ecrivains du Siecle de Louis* xiv.
∥ *Printed in the collection of State-tracts, vol.* 2. *p.* 300.

" A letter

" " A letter to a Diſſenter, upon occaſion of
" his Majeſty's late gracious declaration: of in-
" dulgence," 1687 §.

" An eſſay upon Taxes, calculated for the
" preſent juncture of affairs in England," 1693 ¶.

" Advice to a Daughter."

" The character of a Trimmer."

" Maxims of ſtate applicable to all times *."

" Character of Biſhop Burnet †."

" A ſeaſonable addreſs to both Houſes of Par-
" liament, concerning the Succeſſion, the fears
" of Popery and arbitrary Government," 1681 ‡.

§ *Printed among Somers's tracts, vol.* 2. *p.* 364.
¶ *ib. vol.* 4. *p.* 63.
* *Printed among the works of Villiers Duke of
Buckingham, vol.* 2. *p.* 137.
† *Printed at the end of the Biſhop's Hiſtory of his
own Times.*
‡ *Somers's tracts, ſecond collect. vol.* 3. *p.* 346.

" Cautions

" Cautions for choice of Parliament-men."

" A rough draught of a new model at sea."

" Lord Halifax's historical observations upon
" the reigns of Edward I. II. III. and Rich-
" ard II. with remarks upon their faithful coun-
" fellors and false favorites;" 1689 ‖.

Seven of these pieces were printed together in
octavo, 1704, under the title of " Miscellanies
" by the late Marquis of Halifax."

THOMAS OSBORNE,

DUKE of LEEDS.

IT is by no means neceffary to fay any thing
of this Lord ; He appears in every page of
the reign of Charles the Second. Burnet §

‖ *Harl. Catal. vol.* I. *p.* 438.
§ *vol.* I. *p.* 351.

treats him feverely ; the Peerage vindicates him by a dedication of Dryden, which one muft allow is authority to fuch a book, for nothing can exceed the flattery of a Genealogift, but that of a Dedicator. If the Earl of Danby was far inferior in integrity to Clarendon and Southampton, he was as much fuperior to Shaftsbury and Lauderdale. Leeds was one of thofe fecondary Characters, who having been Firft-Minifter, fubmitted afterwards to act a fubordinate part in an Adminiftration.

His Grace publifhed

" Memoirs relating to the Impeachment of
" Thomas Earl of Danby, [now Duke of
" Leeds] in the year 1678, wherein fome affairs
" of thofe Times are reprefented in a jufter
" light, than has hitherto appeared. With an
" Appendix." Lond. 1710.

" The Earl of Danby's letters in the years
" 1676, 77, and 78; with particular remarks
" upon fome of them," 1710.

HENRY

HENRY BOOTH,

LORD DELAMER,

AND

EARL of WARRINGTON.

IT is remarkable how many of the faireſt names in our ſtory have contributed to grace our memoirs of Litterature. The Lord in queſtion was not only an Author like his Father, but like Him an active inſtrument in a Revolution of Government. Lord Henry, who was thrice impriſoned for his noble love of liberty, and who narrowly eſcaped the fury of James and Jefferies, lived to be commiſſioned by the Prince of Orange to order that King to remove from Whitehall; a meſſage which

he

he delivered with a generous decency.   He was
foon difmiffed by King William to gratify the
Tories ; and died in the forty-fecond year of his
age ; having written a vindication of his dear
Friend, under this title

　　" The late Lord Ruffel's cafe, with obferva-
" tions upon it."

　　" Speech of the honourable Henry Booth
" at Chefter, on his being elected Knight of
" the Shire for that County; March, 1680-1 ‡."

　　" Another Speech," which feems to have been
an addrefs to his county, to-perfuade them to
join the Prince of Orange ‖.

　　" Charges to the Grand Jury in 1691,
" 92, and 93."

‡ *State tracts, vol. 2. p. 147.*
‖ *ib. p. 434.*

　　　　　　　　　　　　　　　　CHARLES

CHARLES SACKVILLE,

EARL of DORSET*.

IF one turns to the authors of the laſt age for the character of this Lord, one meets with nothing but encomiums on his wit and good-nature. He was the fineſt gentleman in the voluptuous court of Charles the Second, and in the gloomy one of King William: He had as much wit as his firſt Maſter, or his co-temporaries Buckingham and Rocheſter, with-

|| *Having omitted him in his place, as being the author only of Speeches and Letters, I ſhall refer my readers for an account of another ornament of this Family,* THOMAS EARL of DORSET, *to Antony Wood, who, vol. 2. p. 155, mentions ſeveral ſpeeches and letters of State of this Lord in print; and whoſe own manly and ſpirited account of his duel with the Lord Bruce is ſufficiently known.*

out

out the royal want of feeling, the Duke's want of principles, or the Earl's want of thought. The latter faid with aftonifhment, " That he " did not know how it was, but Lord Dorfet " might do any thing, and yet was never to " blame."-------It was not that He was free from the failings of humanity, but he had the tendernefs of it too, which made every body excufe whom every body loved, for even the afperity of his verfes feems to have been forgiven to

The beft good Man with the worft-natured Mufe.

This line is not more familiar than Lord Dorfet's own poems to all who have tafte for the genteeleft beauties of natural and eafy verfe, or than his Lordfhip's own bon-mots, of which I cannot help repeating one of fingular humour. Lord Craven was a proverb for officious whifpers to men in power. On Lord Dorfet's promotion, King Charles having feen Lord Craven pay his ufual tribute to him, afked the former what the latter had been faying. The

Earl

Earl replied gravely, " Sir, my Lord Craven " did me the honour to whifper me, but I did " not think it good manners to liften." When He was dying, Congreve, who had been to vifit him, being afked how he had left Him, replied, " Faith, he flabbers more wit than " other people have in their beft health.". His Lordfhip wrote nothing but fmall copies of verfes, moft of which have been collected in the late editions of our Minor Poets; and with the Duke of Buckingham's works are printed ‡ two of Lord Dorfet's poems; as in Prior's pofthumous works ‖ is one called

" The antiquated Coquet."

‡ vol. 2. pages 14, and 56.
‖ vol. 1. p. 170.

WILLIAM

WILLIAM CAVENDISH,

DUKE of DEVONSHIRE:

A Patriot among the Men, galant among the Ladies. His friendſhip with Lord Ruſſel, his free ſpirit, his bravery, duels, honours, amours, are well known, and his epitaph will never be forgotten;.

WILLIELMUS DUX DEVONIÆ,
BONORUM PRINCIPUM SUBDITUS-FIDELIS,
INIMICUS ET INVISUS TYRANNIS.

Of his compoſition we have

" Two Speeches *."

* Printed in Collins's peerage, pages 325, 327.

" A true

" A true copy of a paper delivered by
" the Lord Devonſhire to the Mayor of
" Derby, where he quartered, November 21,
" 1688 †."

" An alluſion to the Biſhop of Cambray's
" ſupplement to Homer, a poem," of which
one or two extracts are to be found in the
peerage ‡.

" Some fragments, in the ſame book."

" An Ode on the death of Queen Mary §."

† *State tracts, vol. 2. p. 438.*
‡ *ubi ſupra, p. 336.*
§ *p. 337.*

JOHN THOMPSON,

LORD HAVERSHAM.

THIS Lord, whom Burnet often mentions curforily, but without thinking him of confequence enough to draw his character, is little known. Being of a republican family, which recommended him *, fays the Author of his life, to the Earl of Anglefey, the Patron of the Diffenters, he married the Daughter of that Earl who recommended him to the good graces of Charles-the Second. The King made him a Baronet, and offered him the Treafurerfhip of the Chambers, which He declined; his principles being yet of a more ftubborn temper than

* *Memoirs of the late Right Honourable John Lord Haverfham, &c. 1711; a fmall pamphlet.*

thofe

those of his Father-in-law. The young Baronet was active againſt the meaſures of the court during the Popiſh reigns, and joined the Prince of Orange, by whom he was made a Baron and Lord of the Admiralty. He † offended the Tory Houſe of Commons who impeached the Whig Lords in 1701; and the Tory Adminiſtration were eager to remove him. However, being diſguſted, as his Biographer ſays ‡, at the promotion of the Earl of Pembroke, " He took all opportunities of oppoſing almoſt " every thing that was advanced by the Court; " *and finding no notice taken of him by the Court,* " *He went on with his reſentment,* and was a " great obſtacle to the occaſional Conformity- " bill, which at that time was voted for by all " who had places of truſt." From this time his Lordſhip ſeems entirely to have abandoned his firſt principles; and to have given himſelf up to the High-Church party, though He continued to go ſometimes to Meetings. His hiſtorian aſcribes this change to the violent meaſures

† *Burnet, vol. 2. p. 278.*
‡ *page 3.*

of

of the Whigs, but after fo candid a confeffion
as he had made above of his Lordfhip's difgufts,
the reader will be apt to think that the *meafures*
of the Whigs were not the fole ftumbling block.
Be that as it may, in 1705, we find || Lord
Haverfham opening the debate againft the Duke
of Marlborough; and in the year 1707, He §
was one of the Lords that attacked the conduct
of the Admiralty. In 1708, " My Lord Haver-
" fham, a great fpeech-maker and publifher
" of his fpeeches *, fays the Dutchefs of
" Marlborough, and who was become the
" mouth of the party for any extraordinary
" alarm, was fent privately by the Tories to the
" Queen to acquaint her with, the difcovery,
" they pretended to have made, of a terrible
" defign formed by the Whigs, to bring over
" one of the Houfe of Hanover, and to force
" this upon Her whether She would or not."
Unluckily this very Lord " had been the Man,

|| *Burnet, p.* 429.
§ *ib. p.* 491.
* *Conduct of the Dowager Duchefs of Marlborough, p.* 163.

" who

" who had moved for the Princefs Sophia's
" coming over, as a thing neceffary for the
" prefervation of the Proteftant religion."

The lift of his Lordfhip's performances is
as follows,

" Obfervations upon feveral occurrencies from
" the beginning of her Majefty's reign [to the
" day of his death] by way of Memoranda."
It contains only three pages, tending to palliate
his change of principles, in which his Lordfhip is not quite fo ingenuous as his Biographer †.

" A vindication of the Earl of Anglefey,
" from being the author of the Memoirs under
" his name." It is contained in a dedication
to King William and Queen Mary, and in a
preface to the Earl of Anglefey's ftate of the
government and kingdom, &c §.

" Speech on the bill to prevent occafional
" Conformity," 1703‖.

† *Printed in the Memoirs of his life, p. 22.*
§ *See before in the article of Anglefey.*
‖ *Vide Memoirs of his life.*   " Ano-

" Another Speech, November 20, 1704 *."

" Speech upon the ſtate of the Nation,"
1705 †.

" A vindication of that Speech ‡."

" Speech againſt the bill for recruiting her
" Majeſty's land-forces ‖."

" Several other Speeches §."

" Account of the proceedings relating to the
" Charge of the Houſe of Commons againſt
" John Lord Haverſham ;" moſt probably writ-

* ibid.
† ibid.
‡ ib. p. 10.
‖ ib. p. 5.
§ ibid.
¶ Somers's tracts, ſecond collect. vol. 4. p. 384.

ANTONY

ANTONY

ASHLEY COOPER,

EARL of SHAFTSBURY,

GRANDSON of the Chancellor, and a Man whose morals were as amiable as the life of the former was hateful. The first was an author only to serve the purposes of the factions in which He was engaged; the writings of the latter breathe the virtues of his mind, for which they are much more estimable than for their style and manner. He delivers his doctrines in ecstatic diction, like one of the Magi inculcating philosophic visions to an eastern auditory!

His

His principal works are publifhed in three volumes, well known by the title of the

" Chara&eriftics of men, manners, opinions, times."

We have befides a fmall colle&ion of his

" Letters to Robert Molefworth, Efq; [now " the Lord Vifcount of that name] with a large " introdu&ion," giving an account of the Earl's public principles,' which were juft what became an Englifhman and a Philofopher. One anec- dote, not mentioned there, but an inftance of his modeft ingenuity, ought to be recorded. Attempting to fpeak on the bill for granting council to prifoners in cafes of high-treafon, He was confounded, and for fome time could not proceed, but recovering himfelf he faid, " What now happened to him, would ferve to " fortify the arguments for the bill———if He, " innocent and pleading for others, was daunted " at the auguftnefs of fuch an affembly, what " muft a man be, who fhould plead before them " for his life?"

" A letter concerning defign *."

* Printed in Bickerton's colleBion, p. 75.

JOHN

JOHN LORD SOMERS,

ONE of thofe divine men, who, like a chapel in a palace, remain unprofaned, while all the reft is tyranny, corruption and folly. All the traditional accounts of him, the hiftorians of the laft age, and it's beft authors reprefent him, as the moft incorrupt Lawyer, and the honefteft Statefman, as a mafter Orator, a Genius of the fineft tafte, and as a Patriot of the nobleft and moft extenfive views; as a Man, who difpenfed bleffings by his life, and planned them for pofterity. He was at once the model of Addifon, and the touchftone of Swift: The one wrote from Him, the other for Him. The former however has drawn a laboured, but diffufe and feeble character of Him in the Freeholder *, neither worthy of the

* Of May 14, 1716.

Author nor his Subject. It is known that my Lord Somers furvived the powers of his under-ftanding: Mr. Addifon fays, "His life indeed " feems to have been prolonged beyond it's na-" tural term under thofe indifpofitions which " hung upon the latter part of it, that he might " have the fatisfaction of feeing the happy fettle-" ment take place, which he had propofed, to " himfelf as the principal end of all his public " labours."------A very wife way indeed of in-terpreting the will of Providence! As if a man was preferved by Heaven in a ftate of dotage, till an event fhould arrive which would make him happy if. He retained his fenfes! Equally in-judicious is another paffage, intended for en-comium, where we are told, "That He gained " great efteem with Queen Anne, who had " conceived many unreafonable prejudices againft " him!" Mr. Addifon might as well have faid, That the Queen had at firft difbelieved, and was afterwards converted to Sir Ifaac Newton's fyftem of Comets: Her Majefty was full as good a judge of Aftronomy, as of Lord Somers's merits. In truth, Mr. Addifon was fometimes as weak a Writer, when he wrote ferioufly, as

he

he was admirable in touching the delicacies of
natural humour. He fays, that my Lord Somers
was often compared with Sir Francis Bacon,
and gives the preference to the former, " *becaufe*
" He, all integrity, did not behave as meanly,
" when profecuted by the Houfe of Commons,
" as the other under conviction of guilt." This
argument is as poor as the panegyric. To argue
from their behaviour, they fhould have been in
fimilar circumftances. If they are to be compared, the fuperior penetration of genius cannot
be denied to Bacon; the virtue will all be
Somers's. If He muft be compared with another Chancellor, it muft not be with Clarendon,
who was more morofe and fevere; had lefs capacity, and a thoufand more prejudices : The great
Chancellor de l'Hofpital feems to refemble
Somers moft in the dignity of his foul and the
elegance of his underftanding.

The momentous times in which He lived,
gave Lord Somers opportunities of difplaying
the extent of his capacity and the patriotifm of
his heart; opportunities as little fought for
the former, as they were honeftly courted and

purfued

purfued for the latter. The excellent balance of our Conftitution, never appeared in a clearer light than with relation to this Lord, who, though impeached by a mifguided Houfe of Commons with all the intemperate folly that at times difgraced the free States of Greece, yet had full liberty to vindicate his innocence and manifeft an integrity, which could never have fhone fo bright, unlefs it had been juridically afperfed. In our Conftitution, Ariftides may be traduced, clamoured againft, and when matter is wanting, fummary addreffes may be propofed or voted † for removing him for ever from the fervice of the Government; but happily the factious and the envious have not a power of condemning by a fhell, which many of them cannot fign.

It was no inglorious part of this great Chancellor's life, that when removed from the adminiftration, his labours were ftill dedicated to the fervice of the government and of his country.

† *As happened in the cafe of Lord Somers ; vide* *Burnet, vol.* 2. *p.* 267.

In

In this situation, above all the little prejudices of a profession, for He had no profession but that of Solon and Lycurgus, he set himself to correct the grievances of the Law, and to amend the vocation He had adorned ‡. The Union of the Kingdoms was projected too by Him ; and it was not to his disgrace, that the Princess, whose prejudices He had conquered, and whose esteem He had gained, offerred him up as one of the first sacrifices on the altar of Utrecht ‖.

Such deathless monuments of his abilities and virtue diminish the regret we should otherwise feel, that though Lord Somers wrote several pieces, we are ignorant even of the titles of many of them ; so little was Fame his object! This modesty is mentioned particularly in the

‡ *ib. p.* 439.

‖ *It is a remarkable, though a trifling anecdote, that this great Man extorted such esteem even from the adverse faction, that Mr. Oliver Leneve, a distinguished Tory, who killed Sir Henry Hobart in a duel, used to toast, " That Her Majesty may " have many Summers." i. e. Somers.*

Freeholder

Freeholder I have quoted. What little I have been able to difcover of his writings are thefe,

"Dryden's Satire to his Mufe*;" this, I think, has been difputed; and indeed the grofs ribaldry of it cannot be believed to have flowed from fo humane and polifhed a nature as Lord Somers's.

"Tranflation of the Epiftle of Dido to "Æneas †."

"Tranflation of Ariadne to Thefeus ‡."

"Tranflation of Plutarch's life of Alci- "biades ∥."

"A juft and modeft vindication of the pro- "ceedings of the two laft Parliaments." 1681.

* *Printed in the third volume of Cogan's edition of the Minor Poets.*
† *Printed in Tonfon's edition. Vide Gen. Dict. vol. 9. p. 283.*
‡ *Vide Life of Lord Somers. A fmall ill-writ- ten pamphlet.*
∥ *Gen. Dict. ubi fupra.*

qu°.

quᵒ. Firſt written by Algernon Sidney, but new, drawn by Somers. ' Publiſhed; in Baldwin's collection of pamphlets in the reign of Charles the Second §.

" Other pieces at that time," not ſpecified ¶.

" A Speech at a conference on the word, " Abdicated *."

" Another on the fame occaſion."

" Speeches at the trial of Lord Preſton †."

" His letter to King William on the partition " treaty ‡."

" His-anſwer to his impeachment."

§ *Burnet,* vol. 1.
¶ *Gen. Dict. p.* 284. *I have met with a ſmall piece, ſaid to be written by Lord Somers, which perhaps was one of the tracts hinted at here ; it is entituled,* " The ſecurity of Engliſhmen's lives, or " the truſt, power and duty of the Grand Juries of " England, explained according to the fundamentals " of the Engliſh government, &c."
* *ibid.*
† *Life, p.* 26.
‡ *Gen. Dict. p.* 286.

" Extracts

" Extracts from two of his letters to Lord
" Wharton *."

" Addresses of the Lords in answer to addresses
" of the Commons †."

" The argument of the Lord Keeper Somers
" on his giving judgment in the Banker's case,
" delivered in the Exchequer-chamber, June
" 23, 1696 ‡."

" A brief History of the Succession collected
" out of the Records, written for the satisfaction
" of the E. of H." In the original copy were
several additions in Lord Somers's hand, from
whence the Editor ascribes it to his Lordship §.

* *ib. p.* 290.
† *Burnet, vol.* 2. *p.* 378.
‡ *Harl. Catal. vol.* 2. *p.* 651.
§ *Vide Somers's tracts, fourth coll. vol.* 4. *p.* 167.
*We have often quoted this work ; it is a collection of
scarce pieces in four sets of four volumes each in
quarto, published by Cogan, from pamphlets chiefly
collected by Lord Somers. A much more valuable
treasure, his Lordship's collection of original papers
and letters, was very lately lost by a fire in the chambers of Mr. Yorke, his Majesty's Sollicitor-general.*

CHARLES

CHARLES MONTAGU,

EARL of HALIFAX,

RAISED himself by his abilities and eloquence in the House of Commons, where
He had the honour of being attacked in conjunction with Lord Somers, and the satisfaction
of establishing his innocence as clearly. Addison
has celebrated this Lord in his account of the
greatest English Poets: Steele has drawn his
character in the dedication of the second volume
of the Spectator, and of the fourth of the
Tatler; but Pope in the portrait of Bufo in
the epistle to Arbuthnot has returned the ridicule,
which his Lordship in conjunction with Prior
had heaped on Dryden's Hind and Panther.
Besides this admirable Travesty, Lord Halifax
wrote

"An

" An anſwer to Mr. Bromley's ſpeech in re-
" lation to the occaſional Conformity-bill *."

" Seaſonable Queries concerning a new Par-
" liament." 1710.

" A poem on the death of Charles the Second."

" The Man of Honour. A poem."

" Ode on the marriage of her Royal Highneſs
" the Princeſs Anne and Prince George of
" Denmark."

" Epiſtle to Charles Earl of Dorſet and Mid-
" dleſex, occaſioned by King William's victory
" in Ireland."

All which, except the Queries, with ſeveral
of his Speeches, have been publiſhed together in
an octavo volume, with " Memoirs of his Lord-
" ſhip's life." 1716.

---

* *Publiſhed in the memoirs of Lord Halifax's*
life.

" Verſes

" Verſes written at Althrop in a blank leaf
" of a Waller, on ſeeing Vandyke's picture of
" Lady Sunderland*."

" Verſes written for the toaſting glaſſes of the
" Kit-Cat Club," 1703. His Lordſhip's are
the heſt of this ſet.

JOHN SHEFFIELD,

DUKE of BUCKINGHAM.

THE life of this Peer takes up fourteen
pages and half in folio in the General
Dictionary, where it has little pretenſions to
occupy a couple :---But his pious Relict was
always purchaſing places for Him, herſelf, and
their Son, in every ſuburb of the Temple of
Fame------a tenure, againſt which of all others

* State-poems, vol. 3. p. 356.

Quo-

Quo-warrantos are fure to take place. The author of the article in the Dictionary calls the Duke one of the moft beautiful profe-writers and greateft poets of this age; which is alfo, he fays, proved by the fineft writers, his cotemporaries------Certificates, that have little weight, where the merit is not proved by the Author's own works. It is certain that his Grace's compofitions in profe have nothing extraordinary in them; his poetry is moft indifferent, and the greateft part of both is already fallen into total neglect. It is faid that He wrote in hopes of being confounded with his predeceffor in the title; but He would more eafily have been miftaken with the other Buckingham, if he had never written at all. He was defcended from Lord Sheffield, the author mentioned above, had a great deal of bravery and underftood a a court. Queen Anne, who undoubtedly had no turn to gallantry, yet fo far refembled her predeceffor Elizabeth, as not to diflike a little homage to her perfon.----This Duke was immediately rewarded on her acceffion, for having made love to her before her marriage. Though attached to the Houfe of Stuart and their principles,

ciples, he maintained a dignity of honour in some points; independent of all connections, for He ridiculed * King James's religion, though He attended him to his Chapel; and warmly took the part of the Catalans againſt the Tory Miniſtry, whom He had helped to introduce to the Queen. His works are publiſhed in two large volumes in quarto. In Prior's poſthumous † works is a little poem to Mrs. Manley on her firſt play, not printed with the reſt of the Duke's compoſitions.

ROBERT HARLEY,

EARL of OXFORD.

THE Hiſtory of this Lord is too freſh in every body's memory to make it requiſite to expatiate upon his character. What blemiſhes

* *Burnet, vol.* I. *p.* 683.
† *vol.* I. *p.* 150.

it had, have been fo feverely cenfured by the
* Affociate of his councils and politics, that a
more diftant obferver has no pretence to enlarge
on them. Befides, as the public conduct of
this Earl, to which alone I know any objections,
was called to fuch ftrict account by perfons of
my name, it would be an ungrateful tafk in
me to renew any difturbance to his afhes. He
is only mentioned here as author of the following tracts,

" An Effay upon public Credit, by Robert
" Harley, Efq;" 1710 †.

" An Effay upon Loans, by the author of the
" Effay on public Credit ‡."

" A vindication of the rights of the Commons
" of England;" faid to be by him, but figned
Humphrey Mackworth ‖.

* Lord Bolinbroke.
† Somers's tracts, vol. 2. p. 1.
‡ ib. p. 10.
‖ ib. fecond coll. vol. 4. p. 313.

EDWARD

EDWARD HOWARD,

EARL of SUFFOLK,

A Lord, who with great inclination to verfify, and fome derangement of his intellects, was fo unlucky as not to have his furor of the true poetic fort. He publifhed two feperate volumes, the firft intituled

" Mifcellanies in profe and verfe by a perfon " of quality." 1725. octavo.

The other, which contains many pieces printed in the former, (both being ufhered by recommendatory verfes) is called

" Mufarum deliciæ, containing Effays upon " Paftoral ; Ideas, fuppofed to be written above " two thoufand years ago by an Afiatic poet, " [who

" [who, it ſeems, wrote in proſe] and who
" flouriſhed under the reign of the Grand Cyrus;
" and Sapphic verſe; by a Nobleman." Printed,
as appears by a date in the middle of the book,
in 1728. The Executors of this Lord conferred
ſome value on his works, by burning a great
number of the copies after his death. Indeed
the firſt volume is not without merit, for his
Lordſhip has tranſplanted whole pages of Milton
into it, under the title of Elegancies.

DANIEL FINCH,

EARL of NOTTINGHAM,

W A S much .aſperſed during his life; but
this was in times on which poſterity
will judge better than we who live ſo near them.
Beſides his ſpeeches, many of which are printed
in a book intituled, " An exact collection of
" the debates of the Houſe of Commons held at
" Weſtminſter,

" Weſtminſter, October 21, 1780," His Lordſhip wrote

" Obſervations upon the State of the Nation,
" in January, 1712-3."

" The anſwer of the Earl of Nottingham,
" to Mr. Whiſton's letter to Him concerning
" the eternity of the Son of God, and of the
" Holy Ghoſt," 1721. The Univerſity of Oxford in full convocation returned his Lordſhip
" *ſolemn thanks* for his moſt noble defence of the
" Chriſtian Faith, &c*."

GEORGE GRANVILLE,

LORD LANSDOWN,

IMITATED Waller; but as that Poet
has been much excelled ſince, a faint copy
of a faint Maſter muſt ſtrike ſtill leſs. It
was fortunate for his Lordſhip, that in an age

* *Vide Peerage in Winchelſea.*

when perfecution raged fo fiercely againft luke-
warm authors, he had an intimacy with the In-
quifitor-General ; how elfe would fuch lines as
this have efcaped the Bathos ?

> "------------when thy Gods
> "*Enlighten* Thee to fpeak their *dark* Decrees *."

A fine edition of his works has been publifhed
in two volumes quarto ; befides which we find

"A letter from a Nobleman abroad to his
"friend in England." 1722†.

"Verfes written on a blank leaf by Lord
"Lanfdown, when he prefented his works to
"the Queen in 1732.

* *Heroic Love, fcene* 1.
† *Somers's tracts, fourth coll. vol.* 4. *p.* 416.
‡ *Dodfley's Mifcellanies, vol.* 1. *p.* 333.

CHARLES

CHARLES BOYLE,

EARL of ORRERY,

OF one of the moſt accompliſhed Houſes in Europe, but the firſt Engliſh Peer of this line that was an author, wrote

"A tranſlation of the life of Lyſander from "Plutarch," publiſhed in the Engliſh edition of that author.

"As you find it, a comedy."

"Some copies of verſes *."

* *Vide Peerage in Boyle, p.* 291; *and Biogr. vol.* 2. *p.* 936.

R 2   "A Latin

" A Latin tranflation of the Epiftles of Pha-
" laris, with the life of Phalaris, and notes to
" that author." This work occafioned the
famous controverfy with Dr. Bentley; a full account of which is given in the life of that great
Man†, who alone, and unworfted, fuftained
the attacks of the brighteft Genius's in the learned World, and whofe fame has not fuffered by
the wit to which it gave occafion.

" Dr. Bentley's differtations on the Epiftles of
" Phalaris and the fables of Æfop, examined by
" the Honourable Charles Boyle, Efq ; " a book
more commonly known by the title of " Boyle
" againft Bentley."

" An Epilogue to his Predeceffor's Altemira,
" and feveral fongs in it."

† *Biogr. vol. 2. p.* 737.

PHILIP

PHILIP

DUKE of *WHARTON*,

LIKE Buckingham and Rochefter, comforted all the grave and dull by throwing away the brighteft profufion of parts on witty fooleries, debaucheries and fcrapes, which may mix graces with a great character, but never can compofe one. If Julius Cæfar had only *rioted* with Cataline, He had never been Emperor of the World. Indeed the Duke of Wharton was not made for conqueft ; He was not equally formed for a Round-houfe and Pharfalia : In one of his ballads he has bantered his own want of heroifm ; it was in a fong he made on being feized by the guard in St.

James's

James's park, for finging the Jacobite air,
The King fhall have his own again,

 " The Duke he drew out half his fword.
 " --------the Guard drew out the reft."

His levities, wit and want of principles, his
eloquence and adventures are too well known,
to be re-capitulated. With attachment to no
party, though with talents to govern any party,
this lively Man changed the free air of Weftminfter for the gloom of the Efcurial, the profpect of
King George's garter for the Pretender's; and
with indifference to all religion, the frolic Lord
who had writ the ballad on the Arch-bifhop
of Canterbury, died in the habit of a Capucin.

It is difficult to give an account of the works
of fo mercurial a Man, whofe library was a
tavern; and women of pleafure his Mufes.
A thoufand fallies of his imagination may have
been loft; he no more wrote for fame than He
acted for it. There are two volumes in octavo
called his life and writings, but containing of
the latter nothing but

      " Seventy-four

" Seventy-four numbers of a periodical paper,
" called the True Briton," and his celebrated

" Speech in the House of Lords, on the third
" reading of the bill to inflict pains and penal-
" ties on Francis Lord Bishop of Rochester,
" May 15, 1723." It is a remarkable anecdote
relating to this Speech, that his Grace, then in
opposition to the Court, went to Chelsea the day
before the last debate on that Prelate's affair,
where acting contrition, He professed being de-
termined to work out his pardon at court by
speaking against the Bishop, in order to which
He begged some hints. The Minister was de-
ceived, and went through the whole cause with
him, pointing out where the strength of the
argument lay and where it's weakness. The
Duke was very thankful, returned to town,
passed the night in drinking, and without going
to bed, went to the House of Lords, where He
spoke *for* the Bishop, re-capitulating in the
most masterly manner, and answering all that
had been urged against Him. His Speech against
the Ministry two years before on the affair of

the

the South-Sea Company had a fatal effect; Earl Stanhope, answering it with so much warmth that he burst a blood-vessel and died.

What little I have found besides written by the Duke, are ...

"The ballads above-mentioned."

"The drinking match at Eden-hall, in imi-
"tation of Chevy-chace." It is printed in the first volume of a Bookseller's miscellany, called, "Whartoniana*."

"Parody of a Song sung at the Opera-house "by Mrs. Tofts, on her leaving the English "stage and returning to Italy†."

His Grace began a play on the story of Mary Queen of Scots, of which I believe nothing remains but these four lines, preserved in the second volume of the same collection;

*p. 19; and in Ralph's miscellaneous poems, p. 55.
† Ralph's poems, p. 131.

"Sure

"Sure were I free, and Norfolk were a prisoner,
"I'd fly with more impatience to his arms,
"Than the poor Israelite gaz'd on the serpent,
"When life was the reward of every look."

Lady Mary Wortley Montagu wrote an epilogue for this play, which is printed in Dodsley's miscellanies.

"A letter in Bickerton's collection," 1745‡.

LORD CHANCELLOR

K I N G,

WAS Nephew of Mr. Locke, who on seeing his treatise in defence of the rights of the Church, persuaded him to apply himself to the Law, to the highest dignity of which He rose.

‡ *page* 29.

We have of his writing

" An eſſay on the rights of the Chriſtian
" Church."

" Inquiry into the conſtitution, diſcipline,
" unity and worſhip of the primitive Church."
1691*.

" Hiſtory of the Apoſtle's creed, with cri-
" tical obſervations on it's ſeveral articles."

" The Speech of Sir Peter King, Knight,
" Recorder of the City of London, at St.
" Margaret's-hill, to the King's moſt excellent
" Majeſty upon his royal entry, September 20,
" 1714."

* *Harl. Catal. vol.* 1. *p.* 107. *Not having
ſeen this piece, I am not ſure it is different from the
foregoing. Nor whether the next mentioned in the
ſame book, p.* 108, *be his Lordſhip's.*

THOMAS

THOMAS LORD *PAGET,*

ELDEST Son of the late Earl of Ux-
bridge, who furvived him, publifhed fome
pieces, particularly

" An effay on human life," in verfe. 1734.
quarto.

" Some reflections upon the adminiftration
" of government:" A pamphlet, 1740.

In both thefe pieces there is much good
fenfe: The former is written in imitation of
Pope's ethic epiftles, and has good lines, but
not much poetry.

S 2   SIR

Sir *ROBERT WALPOLE,*

EARL of ORFORD,

IS only mentioned in this place in his quality of author: It is not proper nor neceſſary for me to touch his character here.------Sixteen unfortunate and inglorious years ſince his removal have already written his Elogium !

About the end of Queen Anne's reign, and

following pamphlets,

" The Sovereign's anſwer to the Glocefter-" ſhire addreſs." *The Sovereign* meaned Charles

Some paragraphs in this piece were inſerted by the Marquis of Wharton.

" Anſwer

" Anſwer to the repreſentation of the Houſe
" of Lords on the ſtate of the navy." 1709.

" The Debts of the Nation ſtated and con-
" ſidered, in four papers." 1710.

" The thirty-five Millions accounted for."
1710.

" A letter from a foreign Miniſter in Eng-
" land to Monſieur Pettecum *." 1710.

" Four letters to a friend in Scotland upon
" Sacheverel's trial." Falſely attributed in the
General Dictionary to Mr. Maynwaring, who
did not write them, though He ſometimes re-
viſed Mr. Walpole's pamphlets.

" A pamphlet † upon the vote of the Houſe
" of Commons with relation to the Allies not
" furniſhing their Quotas."

* See a full account of this Perſon, who was
a volunteer negotiator about the time of the treaty
of Utrecht, in the Memoires de Torcy.

† Lord O. forgot the title, and I have not been
able to recover it.

" A ſhort

"A short History of the Parliament." It is an account of the last Session of the Queen. It was undertaken by desire of Lord Somers and the Whig Lords, on a Thursday, and printed on the Tuesday following. The Dedication was written by a noble Person now living.

"The South-sea Scheme considered."

"A pamphlet against the Peerage-bill." The title lost.

"The Report of the Secret Committee, "June 9, 1715."

"A private letter to General Churchill after "Lord Orford's retirement," was handed about till it got into print ‡.

‡ *It is in Bickerton's collection, p.* 6.

HENRY

HENRY St. JOHN,

VISCOUNT BOLINBROKE,

W ITH the moſt agreable talents in the world and with great parts, was neither happy nor ſuccesful. He wrote againſt the late King, who had forgiven him; againſt Sir Robert Walpole who did forgive him; againſt the Pretender and the Clergy, who never will forgive Him. He is one of our heſt Writers; though his attacks on all governments and all religion [neither of which views He cared directly to own] have neceſſarily involved his ſtyle in a want of perſpicuity. One muſt know the Man before one can often gueſs his meaning.

meaning. He has two other faults which one ſhould not expect in the ſame Writer, much tautology and great want of connection. Beſides his general works publiſhed together ſince his death in five volumes quarto, ſeveral of his letters are preſerved with Pope's, and one or two little pieces of his poetry are extant, for which he had a natural and eaſy turn.

" To Clara;" publiſhed in ſeveral miſcellanies.

" Almahide, a poem *."

" An Epilogue to Lord Orrery's Altemira ‡."

" Prologue to Lord Lanſdown's Heroic Love."

The following political pieces are not republiſhed in his works,

" A letter to the Examiner." 1710.

* Printed in the *Whartoniana*, vol. 2. p. 116.
‡ *Biograph.* vol. 2. 219.

It

It was anfwered by Earl Cowper [of whom I find no other work except his fpeeches] under this title, " A letter to Ifaac Bickerftaffe, Efq; " occafioned by the letter to the Examiner ‖."

" The true copy of a letter from the Right " Honourable the Lord Vifcount Bolinbroke." Printed in the year 1715 §.

" The reprefentation of the Right Honourable " the Lord Vifcount Bolinbroke." Printed in the year 1715 ¶.

JOHN LORD *HERVEY,*

WROTE many pieces of various kinds: His pamphlets are equal to any that ever were written. Publifhed by himfelf were

‖ *Somers's tracts, fourth collect. vol.* 4. *p.* 5.
§ *ib. p.* 253.
¶ *ib. p.* 260.

" Anfwer to the Occafional Writer." 1727.

" The Occafional Writer, Nº. IV. To his
" Imperial Majefty."

" Obfervations on the writings of the Crafts-
" man."

" Sequel of the Obfervations on the writings
" of the Craftfman." 1730.

" Sedition and Defamation difplayed, with a
" Dedication to the Patrons of the Craftfman."

" A fummary account of the ftate of Dun-
" kirk and the negotiations relating thereto;
" in a letter from a Member of Parliament to
" the Mayor of the Borough for which He
" ferves." 1733.

" A letter to the Craftfman on the Game
" of Chefs." 1733.

" The conduct of the oppofition and ten-
" dency of modern Patriotifm." 1734.

" Speech

"Speech on the bill to prevent the settling
"more lands in Mortmain."

"Speech for the Army." 1737.

"A Protest against protesting with reasons."

A paper, intituled, "The Lord's Protest."

"Letter to a Country Gentleman on the re-
"vival of the Salt Duty."

"Account of Queen Anne's bounty."

"Letter to the Bishop of Bangor on his late
"Sermon upon Horses and Asses."

"On the Pyramids, to Mrs. * * *.

"The Quaker's reply to a Country Parson's
"plea against the Quaker's bill for tythes."

"Letter to the Author of Common-Sense,
"or the Englishman's journal of Saturday,
"April 16, 1737."

"Ancient and modern liberty stated and com-
"pared."

"A letter

"A letter from a Country Gentleman to his
"Friend in London, concerning two collections
"of letters and meſſages lately publiſhed be-
"tween the K. Q. Pr. and Prſs."

"An examination of the facts and reaſonings
"contained in a pamphlet, intituled, a letter
"from a Member of Parliament to his Friend
"in the Country, upon the motion to addreſs
"his Majeſty to ſettle 100,000 l. per annum,
"on his Royal Highneſs the Prince of Wales."
1739.

"Some remarks on the Minute Philoſopher."

"Epitaph on Queen Caroline in Latin and
"Engliſh."

"Miſcellaneous thoughts on the preſent poſ-
"ture of affairs." 1742.

"Three ſpeeches on the Gin-act."

"The queſtion ſtated in regard to the Army
"in Flanders."

"A letter to Mr. Cibber on his letter to Mr.
"Pope."

IN VERSE.

" An Epiſtle from a Nobleman to a Doctor of " Divinty." [Dr. Sheridan] 1733.

" To the imitator of the Satire of the ſecond " book of Horace."

" Bolinbroke's addreſs to Ambition, in imita- " tion of the firſt Ode of the fourth book of " Horace." 1737.

" The difference between verbal and practical " Virtue; with a prefatory epiſtle from Mr. " Cibber to Mr. Pope." 1742.

Since his Lordſhip's deceaſe, there have been printed in Dodſley's collection of poems the following by Lord Hervey,

" To Mr. Fox [now Earl of Ilcheſter] writ- " ten at Florence, in imitation of Horace, ode " iv. book 2.†."

" To the ſame from Hampton-Court," 1731‡.

† vol. 3. p. 181.
‡ ib. p. 183.

" Anſwer

" Anfwer to Mr. Hammond's elegy to Mifs
" Dafhwood ‖."

" Four Epiftles in the manner of Ovid §."
That from *Roxana to Philocles* is a miftake,
and fhould be *Roxana to Ufbeck.* That from
Monimia to Philocles is the beft of his Lord-
fhip's poems ; it was defigned for Mifs Sophia
Howe, Maid of Honour, to the Honourable
Antony Lowther.

" Epilogue defigned for Sophonifba ¶."

" An imitation of Horace, addreffed to Lord
" Ilchefter †."

" A love-letter ‡."

" A Satire in the manner of Perfius *."

Lord Hervey left feveral other works in profe
and verfe in manufcript, particularly,

‖ *vol.* 4. *p.* 79.
§ *ib.* 82, *&c.*
¶ *ib. p.* 107.
† *ib. p.* 109.
‡ *ib.* 110.
* *vol.* 5. *p.* 147.

" Agrippina,

" Agrippina, a Tragedy in rhyme."

" Letters to Dr. Middleton on the method
" of filling up the Roman Senate." The Doctor
formed his own fhare in this controverfy into
a treatife publifhed in his works.

" Memoirs from his firft coming to court to
" the death of the Queen."

HENRY LORD HYDE,

AND

CORNBURY.

THIS amiable and difinterefted Lord was
author of a few pamphlets, publifhed
without his name; of fome tragedies, ftill in
manufcript, and of a comedy called

" The miftakes, or the happy refentment."
Given to Mrs. Porter for her benefit, and printed
this year by fubfcription, with a little preface by
the Author of this work.

HORATIO

HORATIO
LORD WALPOLE,

WROTE many political pieces, among which were the following,

"The interest of Great-Britain steadily pur-
"sued. Part I. In answer to a pamphlet in-
"tituled, The case of the Hanover forces." 1743.

"A letter to a certain distinguished patriot and
"applauded orator, on the publication of his
"celebrated speech on the Seaford petition, in
"the Magazines, &c." 1748.

"Complaints of the manufacturers, relating
"to the abuses in marking the sheep and winding
"the wool, &c." 1752.

"Answer to the latter part of Lord Bolin-
"broke's letters on the study of History." MS.

FINIS.

SUPPLEMENT.

HAVING found some scattered passages relating to some other Lords, which scarcely intitle them to places in this Catalogue, and which yet make me doubtful whether they should not be inserted; I chuse for the present to range them here; and if hereafter I discover more evidence relating to them, I shall distribute them in their proper order, supposing this work should be curious enough to call for another edition.

ANTONY BROWN,

VISCOUNT MONTACUTE.

IT is against my rule to reckon peers as authors, of whom nothing is extant but speeches or letters. Indeed where there is a presumption that either were published by the persons themselves, it makes a difference. I should not re-

cord

cord this Lord at all, but from his being mentioned as a writer by Bifhop Tanner for his

  " Speech in the Houfe of Lords againft the " alteration of religion ‡."

LORD CHANCELLOR
HATTON.

WOOD fays ‖, " He wrote, as it is faid, " feveral things pertaining to the Law, " but none of them are extant, only this, if I " may fay it is his, and not his name fet to it " for fale-fake,"

  " A treatife concerning ftatutes or acts of par- " liament, and the expofition thereof." Lond. 1677. octavo.

  " Speeches fpoken during the time of his " Chancellorfhip." M S.

‡ *p.* 131.
‖ *Athenæ, vol.* 1. *p.* 253.

Chriftopher

Chriftopher Lord Hatton, his kinfman and fucceffor, publifhed

" The pfalms of David, with titles and col-
" lects, according to the matter of each pfalm."
Printed at Oxford, 1644, octavo; afterwards
enlarged and publifhed feveral times. Wood
fays‡, that they were compiled by Dr. Jer.
Taylor, though they go under the name of the
Lord Hatton.

THOMAS WENTWORTH,

EARL of STRAFFORD,

IS not recorded here for his fpeeches and letters, thofe chef-d'œuvres of fenfe, of ner-
vous and pathetic eloquence; but on occafion of
an Elegy with fome affecting lines, faid to have
been compofed by him the night before his execution. It has been re-publifhed in the collection § of tracts called Lord Somers's; but in a

‡ ib. p. 254.
§ fecond coll. vol. 2. p. 9.

fubfe-

subsequent † volume we are told that it was a
fiction, avowed afterwards by another person.
Most probably it was not genuine: That Hero
had other ways of venting his scorn than in son-
nets and madrigals. When the Lieutenant of
the Tower offered him a coach, left He should
be torn to pieces by the mob in passing to execution; He replied, " I die to please the people,
" and I will die in their own way." With such
stern indifference to his fate, he was not likely
to debase his dignity by puerile expressions of it.

LORD KEEPER

COVENTRY.

BESIDES re-capitulating several of his
speeches in print, Wood says ‡ he hath
extant

" An answer to the petition against recusants."

† *fourth coll. vol.* I. *p.* 83.
‡ *vol.* I. *p.* 627.

And

And that there goes under his name another piece called,

" Perfect and exact directions to all thofe
" that defire to know the true and juft fees of
" all the offices belonging to the court of Com-
" mon-Pleas, Chancery, &c." Lond. octavo.

JOHN LORD LUCAS.

AS it was burnt by the hands of the hangman, his Lordfhip himfelf probably publifhed his

" Speech in the Houfe of Peers, February
" 22, 1671, upon the reading the fubfidy-bill
" the fecond time in the prefence of his Ma-
" jefty §." In the ftate-poems I find one ¶, alluding to this fpeech, called " Lord Lucas's
" Ghoft."

§ *State-tracts, vol.* 1. *p.* 454.
¶ *vol.* 1. *p.* 173.

                                    ROBERT

ROBERT SPENCER,

EARL of SUNDERLAND,

HAVING been loaded with variety of accufations for the lengths He had gone in countenancing Popery to flatter King James, and with betraying him afterwards to the Prince of Orange, publifhed a vindication of his conduct called

" The Earl of Sunderland's letter to a friend " in the country, &c. March 23, 1689 ¶."

JOHN LORD *JEFFERIES,*

SON of the noted Chancellor. I find two little pieces afcribed to this Lord in the collection of State-poems in four volumes quarto, one is called

¶ *Somers's tracts, vol.* I. *p.* 602.

" A

" A Fable †." The other ¶

" A burlefque tranflation of an Elegy on the
" Duke of Gloucefter."

ROBERT DUDLEY,

DUKE OF

NORTHUMBERLAND,

CALLED the natural Son, probably the
legitimate Son of the great Earl of Leicef-
ter ; having been deprived of his birth-right,
and never acknowledged as a Peer of England,
could not with propriety be claffed among that
order : Yet He was too great an honour to his
country to be omitted ; and it is the duty of the
meaneft Hiftorian, and his felicity to have in his
power, to do juftice to the memory of the de-
ferving, which falls not within the compafs of
particulars to procure to the living. The Author of thofe curious lives of the Dudleys in the

† *vol.* 2. *p.* 241.
¶ *vol.* 3. *p.* 342.   Biographia

Biographia has already retrieved the fame of this
extraordinary perfon from oblivion; and therefore I fhall touch but very few particulars of
his ftory. He * was educated under Sir Thomas
Chaloner, the accomplifhed governor of Prince
Henry, and diftinguifhed his youth by martial
atchievements, and by ufeful difcoveries in the
Weft-Indies. But it was the Houfe of Medici,
thofe patrons of learning and talents, who fof-
tered this enterprizing fpirit, and who were am-
ply rewarded for their munificence by his pro-
jecting the free-port of Leghorn. He flourifhed
in their court and in that of the Emperor, who
declared him Duke of Northumberland, a Duke-
dom remarkably confirmed to his Widow, whom
Charles the Second created Duchefs Dudley.
Antony Wood fays †, "The Duke was a com-
" pleat gentleman in all fuitable employments, an
" exact feaman, an excellent architect, mathe-
" matician, phyfician, chymift, and what not?
" He was a handfome perfonable man, tall of
" ftature, red-haired, and of admirable comport,
" and above all noted for riding the great-horfe,

* *Wood*, vol. 2. p. 126.

† *ib. p.* 27.

"for

" for tilting, and for his being the firſt of all,
" that taught a Dog to fit in order to catch
" partridges." The ſame author gives this liſt
of his works,

" Voyage to the iſland of Trinidada and the
" coaſt of Paria, 1594, 1595*."

" Del arcano del mare, &c." Firenze 1630,
1646 ; in two volumes folio ; full of mathema-
tical cuts, ſea-charts, fortifications, &c.

" A diſcourſe to correct the exorbitances of
" Parliaments, and to enlarge the King's re-
" venue†. Written in the year 1613." This
is the only uncommendable performance of our
Author's life, and as it was attended by an extraordinary anecdote, the Reader is deſired to take
a little notice of it, one very particular circum-
ſtance having never, as I know, been remarked.
This paper, by which Dudley had ſought to in-
gratiate himſelf with James the Firſt, conclud-
ing no method ſo eaſy or ſure for recovering his

---

* See Hakeluyt's third volume of Engliſh voyages,
p. 574.

† Ruſhworth, vol. 1. in the appendix, p. 12.

own right as to inftruct the King how to ufurp
upon the rights of his fubjects, this paper had long,
lain neglected; but in the year 1628, an Information was filed by Sir Robert Heath, Attorney-
general, in the Star-chamber, againft the Earls
of Bedford, Somerfet, and Clare, Sir Robert
Cotton, John Selden and Oliver St. John, for
difperfing this fhamelefs libel. Foulis § would
afcribe this publication to the Patriots, who
meaned to make the King odious; a moft improbable charge, and not at all confirmed by
what really happened afterwards, when it was
re-publifhed under the title of " Strafford's plot."
There is greater reafon to prefume that this attack on parliaments was not made without the
connivance of the court, at leaft was not dif-
agreable to it, the Attorney-general receiving
orders, in the middle of the profecution, to dif-
mifs the caufe, on pretence that his Majefty,
was willing to extend his royal lenity to his fubjects on the birth of a Prince, of whom the Queen
was juft delivered. The remarkable incident un-
noticed, was the Earl of Somerfet being involved
in this trial, that haughty and fallen Favorite,

§ *Hift. of plots,* book I. *p.* 68.

generally

generally fuppofed to have dragged out the re-
mainder of his life in infamy and obfcurity, but
who here appears engaged in ftate-intrigues
with fome of the greateft Lords at that period.

"Catholicon." A phyfical book. He alfo
difcovered a purging powder, which paffes under
the name of a Phyfician who wrote a book on the
virtues of it, and dedicated it to the Duke.
Confidering how enterprizing and dangerous a
Minifter He might have made, and what variety
of talents were called forth by his misfortunes,
it feems to have been happy both for the Duke
and his country, that He was unjuftly deprived
of the honours to which his birth gave him
pretenfions.

PEERESSES,

PEERESSES.

*A*S a thick quarto § volume has been publiſhed within theſe few years of ſuch illuſtrious Women as have contributed to the Republic of Letters, I ſhall be very brief on this head, having little to add to what that Author has ſaid.

MARGARET,

COUNTESS of RICHMOND

AND

DERBY,

*T*HE Mother of Henry the Seventh, to whom She ſeems to have willingly ceded her *no* right to the Crown, while She employed

§ *Memoirs of ſeveral Ladies of Great-Britain, who have been celebrated for their writings, &c. by George Ballard,* 1752.

herſelf

herfelf in founding Colleges, and in acts of more real devotion and goodnefs than generally attend fo much fuperftition. While She was yet young and a rich heirefs, the great Duke of Suffolk, Minifter to Henry the Sixth, or rather to Queen Margaret, follicited her in marriage for his Son, though the King himfelf woed Her for his half-brother Edmund. On fo nice a point the good young Lady advifed with an elderly Gentle-woman, who thinking it too great a decifion to take upon herfelf, recommended her to St. Nicholas, who whipping on fome epifcopal robes, appeared to her and declared in favour of Edmund. The old Gentlewoman, I fuppofe, was dead, and St. Nicholas out of the way, for we hear nothing of the Lady Margaret con-fulting either of them on the choice of two other Hufbands after the death of Earl Edmund, by whom She had King Henry. Sir Henry Stafford, the fecond, bequeathed to his Son-in-law, a trappur of four new horfe harnifh of vel-vet; and his Mother the Duchefs of Bucking-ham, in confideration of the Lady Margaret's great affection for litterature gave her the fol-lowing legacy by her will, " To my daughter

Richmond

"Richmond a book of English, being a legend
" of faints; a book of French called, 'Lucun;
" another book of French, of the epiftles and
" gofpels; and a primmer with clafps of filver
" gilt, covered with purple velvet *."

Her virtues are exceedingly celebrated : "Her
" humility was fuch that She would often fay,
" on condition that the Princes of Chriftendom
" would combine themfelves and march againft
" the common enemy the Turks, She would
" moft willingly attend them and be their laun-
" drefs in the camp †." And for her chaftity,
the reverend Mr. Baker, who re-publifhed Bifhop Fifher's funeral fermon on her, informs us,
" That in her laft hufband's days She obtained a
" licence of him to live chafte, whereupon She
" took upon her the vow of celibacy."-------A
boon as feldom requefted, I believe, of a third
hufband, as it probably would be eafily granted.

This Princefs publifhed
" The mirroure of golde for the finfull foule,
" tranflated from a French tranflation of a book

* *Dugdale.*
† *Camden's remains, p.* 271. *edit.* 1651.

" called,

"called, Speculum aureum peccatorum." Em-
prynted at London, in Fletftrete, at the figne
of St. George by Richard Pynfon, quarto, with
cuts on vellum ‡.

"Tranflation of the fourth book of Dr. J.
"Gerfon's treatife of the imitation and follow-
"ing the blefled life of our moft merciful Saviour
"Chrift." Printed at the end of Dr. William
Atkinfon's Englifh tranflation of the three firft
books, 1504.

She alfo by her Son's command and authority
"Made the orders [yet extant] for great eftates
"of Ladies and noble Women, for their pre-
"cedence, attires, and wearing of barbes at
"funerals over the Chin and under the
"fame ‖."

‡ *Ballard, p. 16.*
‖ *Ballard aud Sandford.*

JOANNA

JOANNA

LADY *BERGAVENNY.*

IN Lord Oxford's library was the following
book*,

" The monument of matrons, containing
" feven feveral lamps of virginitie or diftinct
" treatifes, compiled by Thomas Bently," black
letter, no date. In the beginning was a note
written by the reverend Mr. Baker, faying that
this book contained feveral valuable pieces or
prayers, by Queen Katherine, Queen Elizabeth,
the Lady Abergavenny and others. If I guefs
right, this Lady Abergavenny was Joanna,
daughter of Thomas Fitz-Alan Earl of Arundel,
wife of George Lord Bergavenny, who died in
the twenty-feventh of Henry the Eighth, and
Niece of that bright reftorer of Litterature,

* *Harl. Catal. vol.* i. *p.* 100.

Antony

Antony Earl Rivers. If my conjecture is juft, She was probably the Foundrefs of that noble fchool of female learning, of which [with herfelf] there were no lefs than four Authoreffes in three defcents, as will appear by this fhort table, and by the fubfequent account of thofe illuftrious Ladies:

Thos. Fitz-Alan Earl of Arundel,

William,   Joanna,
                           G. Ld. Bergavenny,

Henry = Mary Arundel,

Joanna,   Mary,
Lord Lumley.   T. D. of Norfolk.

LADY *JANE* GRAY.

THIS admirable young Heroine fhould per-haps be inferted in the Royal Catalogue, rather than here, as She was no Peerefs; but having omitted her there, as She is never ranked in the lift of Kings and Queens, it is impoffible entirely to leave out the faireft ornament of her Sex. It is remarkable that her Mother [like the Countefs of Richmond before-mentioned] not only waved her * fmall pretenfions in favour

of

* It is very obfervable how many defects concurred in the title of this Princefs to the Crown. I. Her Defcent was from the younger Sifter of Henry the Eighth, and there were defcendents of the Elder living, whofe claim indeed had been fet afide by the power given by parliament to King Henry to regulate the fucceffion.------A power, which not being founded on national expedience, could be of no force: And additionally invalidated by that King having by the fame authority fettled the crown preferably on his own daughters, who were both living. II. Her Mother, from whom alcne Jane could derive any right, was alive. III. That Mother was young enough to have other children [not being paft thirty-one † at the death of King Edward] and if She had born a Son, his right, prior to that of his Sifter, was inconteftable. IV. Charles Brandon, father of the Duchefs of Suffolk, had married one woman while contracted to another; but was divorced to fulfil his promife: The repudiated Wife

† See Vertue's print of this Duchefs and her fecond Hufband, where her age is faid to be thirty fix, in 1559.

was

'of' her daughter, but bore her train when She made her public entry into the Tower‡.

Of this lovely Scholar's writing we have

" Four Latin epiftles," three to Bullinger, and one to her Sifter the Lady Catherine; printed in a book called, " Epiftolæ ab Ecclefiæ " Helveticæ reformatoribus, vel ad eos fcriptæ, " &c." Tiguri. 1742. octavo. The fourth was written the night before her death in a Greek Teftament in which She had been reading, and which She fent to her Sifter.

" Her conference with Feckenham Abbot of " Weftminfter, who was fent to convert Her " to Popery ∥."

was living, when he married. Mary Queen of *France, by whom he had the Duchefs. V. If how-* *ever Charles Brandon's firft marriage fhould be* *deemed null, there is no fuch plea to be made in* *favour of the Duchefs Frances herfelf, Henry Duke* *of Suffolk, father of Jane, being actually married* *to the fifter of the Earl of Arundel, whom he di-* *vorced without the leaft grounds, to make room for* *his marriage with Frances.*

‡ *Strype's memorials, vol.* 3. *p.* 2.

∥ *Ballard, p.* 105.

" A letter

" A letter to Dr. Harding, her Father's chap-
" lain, who had apoſtatized §."

" A prayer for her own uſe during her impri-
" ſonment ¶."

" Four Latin verſes written in priſon with a
" pin *."

" Her ſpeech on the ſcaffold †."

Hollingſhed and Sir Richard Baker ſay She
wrote divers other things, but not where they
are to be found.   Bale ‡ adds to the above-
mentioned

" The complaint of a ſinner."

" The duty of a chriſtian."

      Fox ‖ mentions
" A letter to her father."

§ *Printed in the Phænix, vol. 2. p. 28.*
¶ *Vide Fox's acts and monuments.*
* *Ballard, p. 116.*
† *ib. p. 114.*
‡ *p. 110.*
‖ *Fox, p. 1420.*   *MARY*

M A R Y

COUNTESS of *ARUNDEL*,

DAUGHTER of Thomas Lord Arundel of Wardour, married firſt to Robert Ratcliff Earl of Suſſex, and afterwards to Henry Fitz-Alan Earl of Arundel, as may be ſeen in the preceding table. She tranſlated from Engliſh into Latin,

"Sententias & præclara facta Alexandri Se-
"veri imperatoris;" and dedicated it to her father. Extant in manuſcript in the King's library ‡.

"De ſtirpe & familiâ Alexandri Severi, &
"de ſignis quæ ei portendebant imperium."

‡ *Vide Caſley's catalogue, p.* 196.

From

From Greek into Latin

" Selectas fententias feptem fapientum Græ-
" corum."

" Similitudines ex Platonis, Ariftotelis, Senecæ
" & aliorum Philofophorum libris. collectas."
Dedicated to her father ‖.

Learning had now taken a confiderable flight
fince the days of Edward the Fourth: Sir
Thomas More mentions it as very extraordinary
that Jane Shore could read and write.

JOANNA LADY LUMLEY,

ELDEST daughter of the Lady laft-mentioned, tranflated from the original into
Latin

" Ifocrates's oration called Archidamus."
Manufcript in the King's library.

‖ *Vide Tanner's biblioth. Brit. p. 50, and Cafley
ubi fupra.*

" The

"The second and third orations to Nicocles." Dedicated to her father †.

"A fourth, intituled Evagoras." Dedicated to the fame. In the fame place.

From Greek into Englifh

"The Iphigenia of Euripides." Extant in the fame place.

M A R Y

DUCHESS of NORFOLK *,

YOUNGER daughter of the Countefs of Arundel, and firft wife of Thomas Duke of Norfolk, who was beheaded on account of the Queen of Scots, tranflated from Greek

"Certain ingenious fentences collected out of "various authors :" Dedicated to her father ‡.

† *ibid.*
* *She died in* 1557.
‡ *In the King's library.* MARY

MARY

COUNTESS of PEMBROKE,

THE celebrated Sifter of Sir Philip Sidney, wrote

" Poems and tranflations in verfe of feveral " pfalms," faid to be preferved in the library at Wilton †.

"A difcourfe of life and death, written in " French by Philip Mornay, done into Englifh " by the Countefs of Pembroke, dated May 13, " 1590, at Wilton." Printed at London for H. Ponfonby, 1600, 12mo.

" The Tragedie of Antonie, done into Eng- " lifh by the Countefs of Pembroke." Lond. 1595, 12mo.

† *Ballard, p.* 260.

ELIZABETH

ELIZABETH
LADY RUSSEL,

OF a family as learned as the Fitz-Alans, was third daughter of Sir Antony Cooke, and Sifter of the Ladies Burleigh and Bacon, whofe erudition is fufficiently known. She was married, firft to Sir Thomas Hobby, Embaffador from Queen Elizabeth at Paris, where he died 1566; and fecondly to John Lord Ruffel, Son of Francis, the fecond Earl of Bedford. She furvived both her Hufbands, and wrote Greek, Latin and Englifh epitaphs in verfe for them and others of her relations. It is her daughter by her fecond Hufband, whofe effigy is foolifhly fhown in Weftminfter-Abbey, as killed by the prick of a needle.

Lady Ruffel tranflated out of French into Englifh

"A way of reconciliation of a good and learn-
" ed man, touching the true nature and sub-
" stance of the body, and blood of Christ in the
" sacrament." Printed 1605; and dedicated to
her daughter Anne Ruffel, wife of Lord Henry
Herbert, heir of Edward Earl of Worcester;
with Latin and English verses.

Ballard has printed †

" A letter to Lord Burleigh about the extra-
" vagance of her youngest Son."

E L I Z A B E T H

COUNTESS of LINCOLN,

DAUGHTER and coheiress of Sir Henry
Knevet, and wife of Thomas Earl of
Lincoln, wrote

† *ib. p.* 195.

"The

" The Countefs of Lincoln's nurferie ‡."
Oxf. 1621. 4°. Addreffed to her daughter-in-law Bridget Countefs of Lincoln. She fpeaks of it as the firft of her printed works; but I can find no account of any other.

A N N E

COUNTESS of DORSET

AND

PEMBROKE.

THIS high-born and high-fpirited Lady was Heirefs of the Cliffords Earls of Cumberland, and was firft married to Richard Earl of Dorfet, whofe life and actions She celebrated. Her fecond match was not fo happy, being foon parted from her Lord, that memora-

‡ *ib.* 267. *Wood afcribes this piece to one Dr. Lodge, vol. 2. p.* 498.

Z 2

ble

ble fimpleton † Philip Earl of Pembroke and Montgomery, with whom Butler has fo much diverted himfelf. Anne the Countefs was remarkably religious, magnificent and difpofed to letters. She erected a pillar in the county of Weftmorland on the fpot where She took the laft leave of her Mother, a monument to her tutor Samuel Daniel, the poetic hiftorian, another to Spenfer, founded two hofpitals, and repaired or built feven churches and fix caftles ‡. She wrote

" Memoirs of her hufband Richard Earl of " Dorfet:" Never printed.

" Sundry memorials of herfelf and her pro-
" genitors."

---

† *The firft wife of this Earl was Sufan daughter of the Earl of Oxford. I find a book fet forth in her name called,* " *The Countefs of Montgomery's* " *Eufebia, expreffing briefly the Soul's praying* " *robes, by Newton,* 1620." *Vide Harl. Catal. vol.* I. *p.* 100.

‡ *Vide Ballard, and Memorials of worthy perfons, p.* 92, *and* 94.

And

And the following letter to Sir Joseph Williamſon, Secretary of State to Charles the Second, who having ſent to nominate to her a Member for the borough of Appleby, She returned this reſolute anſwer, which though printed in another place ‖, is moſt proper to be inſerted here:

"I Have been bullied by an Uſurper, I have been neglected by a Court, but I will not be dictated to by a Subject: Your Man ſha'n't ſtand.

ANNE DORSET,
PEMBROKE and MONTGOMERY."

MARGARET

DUCHESS of NEWCASTLE.

HAVING already taken notice of her Grace in the courſe of this work, I ſhall here only give a liſt of her works, which fill many folios.

‖ *The World, vol.* 1. *numb.* xiv.   "The

" The World's Olio.

" Nature's picture drawn by Fancy's pencil
" to the life." " In this volume," says the
title, " are several feigned stories of natural
" descriptions, as comical, tragical and tragi-
" comical, poetical, romantical, philosophical,
" and historical, &c. &c." Lond. 1656. folio.
One may guess how like this portrait of Nature
is, by the fantastic bill of the features.

" Orations of divers sorts, accomodated to
" divers places." Lond. 1662. fol.

" Plays." Lond. 1662.

" Philosophical and physical opinions." Lond.
1663. fol.

" Observations upon experimental philosophy.
" To which is added the description of a new
" world." Lond. 1668. folio. One Mr. James
Bristow began to translate some part of these
philosophic discourses into Latin.

" Philoso-

" Philofophical letters." Lond. 1664. fol.

" Poems and phancies." Lond. 1664. fol.

" Sociable letters." Lond. 1664. fol.

" The life of the Duke her hufband, &c."
Lond. 1667. fol. It was tranflated into Latin.

" Plays never before printed." Lond. 1668. fol.

Her plays alone are nineteen in number, and
fome of them in two parts. One of them,
" The blazing world," is unfinifhed, her Grace
[which feems never elfe to have happened to her]
" finding her genius not tend to the profecution
" of it." To another called, " The Prefence,"
are nine and twenty fupernumerary fcenes. In
another, " The unnatural Tragedy," is a whole
fcene written againft Camden's Britannia: Her
Grace thought, I fuppofe, that a geographic
fatire in the middle of a play was mixing the
utile with the *dulci*. Three volumes more in
folio of her poems are preferved in manufcript.
Whoever has a mind to know more of this fertile
pedant, will find a detail of her works in Ballard's memoirs, from whence I have taken this
account. *ANNE*

A N N E

COUNTESS of WINCHELSEA,

AN efteemed Poetefs, is recorded, with fome of her poems in the General Dictionary. Her

"Poem on the fpleen," was printed in Gildon's mifcellany, 1701. octavo. Rowe addreffed one to her on the fight of it.

Her poems were printed at London, 1713, octavo; with a tragedy never acted, called, "Ariftomenes." *

---

* *In the mifcellany [vol. 2.] called,* "*Buckingham's works,*" *I find a very filly poem afcribed to a* LADY SANDWICH. *This fhould be the Lady lately deceafed at Paris, daughter of the celebrated Earl of Rochefter: But She inherited too much wit to have written fo ill.*

A copy

A copy of her verfes to Mr. Pope are printed before the old edition of his works; and two others of his and hers are in the General Dictionary.

Another little poem in Prior's pofthumous works *.

A great number of her poems are faid to be extant in manufcript †.

S A R A H

DUCH^{fs.} of MARLBOROUGH.

IT is feldom the Public receives information on Princes and Favorites from the fountain-head: Flattery or invective is apt to prevert the relations of others. It is from their own pens alone, whenever they are fo gracious,

* vol. 1. p. 20.
† General Dict. vol. 10. Ballard, p. 431.

like the Lady in queſtion, as to have *a paſſion for fame and approbation**, that we learn exactly, how trifling and fooliſh and ridiculous their views and actions were, and how often the miſchief they did proceeded from the moſt inadequate cauſes. We happen to know indeed, though he was no author, that the Duke of Buckingham's repulſes in very impertinent amours, involved King James and King Charles in national quarrels with Spain and France. From her Grace of Marlborough we may collect, that Queen Anne was driven to change her Miniſtry, and in conſequence, the fate of Europe, becauſe She dared to affect one bed-chamber woman, as She had done another. The Ducheſs could not comprehend how the Couſins Sarah Jennings and Abigail Hill could ever enter into competition, though the One did but kneel to gather up the clue of favour, which the other had haughtily toſſed away ; and which She could not recover by putting The Whole Duty of Man into the Queen's hands to teach her Friendſhip†.

* *Vide her apology, p.* 5.
† *ib. p.* 268.

This

This favorite Duchefs, who like the proud Duke of Efpernon, lived to brave the Succeffors in a court where She had domineered, wound up her capricious life, where it feems She had begun it, with an apology for her Conduct. The piece, though weakened by the prudence of thofe who were to correct it, though maimed by her Grace's own corrections, and though great part of it is rather the annals of a ward-robe than of a reign, yet has ftill curious anec-dotes, and a few of thofe fallies of wit which fourfcore years of arrogance could not fail to produce in fo fantaftic an underftanding. And yet by altering her memoires as often as her will, She difappointed the public as much as her own family. However, the cheif objects remain; and one fees exactly how Europe and the back-ftairs took their places in her imagination and in her narrative. The Revolution left no im-preffion on her mind but of Queen Mary turn-ing up bed-cloaths; and the Proteftant Hero, of but a felfifh glutton who devoured a difh of peas from his Sifter-in-law. In fact, events paffing through the medium of our paffions. muft ftrike different beholders in very different lights : Had

Marlborough

Marlborough himfelf written his own hiftory from his heart as the partner of his fortunes did, He would probably have dwelt on the diamond fword, which the Emperor gave him, and have fcrupuloufly told us how many carrats each diamond weighed. I fay not this in detraction from his merits and fervices: It is from our paffions and foibles that Providence calls forth it's great purpofes. If the Duke could have been content with an hundred thoufand pounds, he might poffibly have ftopped at the taking of Leige: As He thirfted for a million, He penetrated to Hockftet.

Mrs. Abigail Hill is not the only perfon tranfmitted to pofterity with marks of the Duchefs's refentment. Lord Oxford, *Honeft Jack Hill*, *the ragged Boy*, *the Quebec-General*, and others make the fame figure in her hiftory that they did in her mind.----------Sallies of paffion not to be wondered at in One who has facrificed even the private letters of her Miftrefs and Benefactrefs!

We

We have nothing of her Grace's writing but the

"Apology for the conduct of the Dowager
"Duchefs of Marlborough from her firft com-
"ing to court to the year 1710, in a letter from
"herfelf to my Lord.* * * *." Lond. 1742.

FRANCES

DUCHESS of SOMERSET,

HAD as much tafte for the writings of others, as modefty about her own.

SCOTCH

SCOTCH AUTHORS.

*I*T is not my purpose to give an exact account of the Royal and Noble Authors of Scotland: I am not enough versed in them to do justice to Writers of the most accomplished Nation in Europe; the Nation to which, if any one Country is endowed with a superior partition of sense, I should be inclined to give the preference in that particular.

ters is what has occurred to me accidentally. Many Natives of each kingdom are far better qualified to compleat the Catalogue, to which I only mean to contribute some hints. Even in the English List I pretend to no merit but in the pains I have taken, and that with too much hurry.

JAMES THE FIRST.*

W ROTE

      "On his future Wife," one book.

                                 "Scotch

* For this account of the Scotch Kings see Tanner, p. 426. I have omitted the second James, whom

" Scotch fonnets," one book.   One of them,
" A lamentation while in England," is in manufcript in the Bodleian library, and praifes Gower
and Chaucer exceedingly.

"Rythmos Latinos." lib. 1.

" On Mufic."

JAMES THE FOURTH,

WROTE

"On the Apocalypfe."

JAMES THE FIFTH,

WROTE the celebrated ballad called

" Chrift's Kirk on the green."

*whom the Bifhop makes an author becaufe. edidit
edictum pacificatorium : A Conftable that reads
the Riot-act is as much intituled to that denomina-
tion.*

MARY

MARY.

IT would be idle to dwell on the ftory of this Princefs, too well known from having the misfortune to be born in the fame age, in the fame ifland with, and to be handfomer than Elizabeth. Mary had the weaknefs to fet up a claim to a greater kingdom than her own without an army; and was at laft reduced by her crimes to be a * Saint in a religion, which was oppofite to what her rival profeffed out of policy. Their different talents for a Crown appeared even in their paffions as Women: Mary deftroyed her Hufband for killing a Mufician that was her galant; and then married her Hufband's affaffin. Elizabeth difdained to marry her Lovers,

---

* In the Church of the Celeftins at Paris it is faid on the tomb of Francis the Second, " That it is proof " enough of his beatitude, that he had the Martyr " Mary Stuart to his wife."

and

and put one of them to death for prefuming too much on her affection. The Miftrefs of David Rizio could not but mifcarry in a conteft with the Queen of Effex. As handfome as She was, Sixtus the Fifth never wifhed to pafs a night with Mary.-------She was no mould to caft Alexanders !

Hiftorians agree in the variety of her accomplifhments. She altered a Latin diftich which She found in the fragments of Cæfar, and wrote on a pane of Glafs at Buxton wells †,

"Buxtona, quæ calidæ celebraris nomine lymphæ,
   "Fortè mihi pofthâc non adeunda, vale!" ‖

As She did this diftich in a window at Fotheringay,

   "From the top of all my truft,
   "Mifhap has laid me in the duft ‡."

   She is reported to have written ‖

"Poems on various occafions," in the Latin, French and Scotch languages.

† *Ballard.*
‡ *ibid.*
‖ *Tanner.*

"Royal

"Royal advice to her Son," in two books.

Among the Latin § poems of Sir Thomas Chaloner is a copy of verses-said to be translated from some French ones written by this Queen, and sent, with a diamond curiously set, to Queen Elizabeth.

A great number of her original letters are preserved in the King of France's library, in the Royal, Cottonian and Ashmolean libraries here: As many others are in print, *viz.*

"Eleven to Earl Bothwell," translated from the French by Edward Simmons, of Christ-Church, Oxford; and printed at Westminster, 1726.

" Ten more ¶, with her answers to the arti-" cles against her."

" Six more," in Anderson's collections.

" Another," in the appendix to her life by Dr. Jebb.

§ *Page* 353, *at the end of his book de Repub. Anglor. inftaur.*

¶ *In Haynes's State-papers.*

And

And some others dispersed among the works of Pius the Fifth, Buchanan, Camden, Udal and Sanderson.

LORD CHANCELLOR

MAITLAND,

CREATED Lord Maitland by James the Sixth, to whom he had been Secretary of State, was famous for his

"Latin epigrams †."

WILLIAM ALEXANDER,

EARL of STIRLING,

WAS a very celebrated Poet, and greatly superior to the style of his age. His works are printed in folio: The cheif of which are four Tragedies in alternate rhyme.——The first grant of Nova Scotia was made to this Lord.+

† *Vide Bacon-papers, vol. 1. p. 295.*

Sir *ROBERT KERR,*
EARL of ANCRAM.

I Find a † short, but very p   copy of verses
from him to Drummond of Hawthornden,
one of the best modern historians, and no mean
imitator of Livy.

JOHN LORD *NEPER,*

BARON of Marcheston, renowned for his
mathematic and logarithmic knowledge,
and author of the celebrated invention called
Neper's bones, drew up an account of his other
discoveries in a book called ‡

" Secret inventions profitable and necessary in
" these days for defence of this island, and with-

† *Vide at the end of Drummond's works.*
‡ *Bacon-papers, vol.* 2. *p.* 28.
                                        " standing

" ftanding of ftrangers, enemies of God's truth
" and religion." Some of thefe projects found
a little, like the Marquis of Worcefter's; one
is a burning-glafs to deftroy fhips; another, a
method for failing under water.

JAMES
DUKE HAMILTON,

THIS Nobleman, fo well known by his
politics and tragic end, is feldom confidered in the light of an Author, yet ‖ Antony
Wood mentions the following pieces,

Preface to a book intituled, " General de-
" mands concerning the late Covenant, &c."
1638. quarto.

" Various letters."

" Conferences, advices, anfwers, &c." publifhed in Burnet's lives of the Dukes of
Hamilton.

HENRY CARY,

LORD FALKLAND.

SCotland and England have each pretensions to this conspicuous line, of which Four succeffively were Authors †. England gave them origine, Scotland their title. Henry is said by the Scotch peerage to have been made Comptroller of the Houfhold and a Peer by King James, for being the firft who carried him the news of the death of Queen Elizabeth; but that is a blunder: Robert Carey Earl of Monmouth was that Meffenger. Lord Falkland was Mafter of the Jewel-office to Elizabeth, and was made Knight of the Bath at the creation of Prince Henry, and Lord Lieutenant of Ire-

† *It is to preferve this chain entire, that I have chofen to place thefe four Lords together, though they ought to have been intermixed with the reft in this lift, according to the periods in which they lived.*

land,

land, from which he was removed with difgrace by the intrigues of the Papifts; yet his honour was afterwards entirely vindicated ‡. He is remarkable for an invention to prevent his name being counterfeited, by artfully concealing in it the fucceffive year of his age, and by that means detecting a Man who had not obferved fo nice a particularity ‖. He had an excellent character; and is faid to have written many things which never were publifhed, except

"The Hiftory of the moft unfortunate Prince, "King Edward the Second; with choice poli- "tical obfervations on him and his unhappy "Favorites, &c." Found among his papers, and printed 1680, folio and octavo.

‡ *Biogr. vol. 2.*

‖ *Loyd's State-worthies, p.* 938. *This little circumftance was thought not unworthy of repetition at a time when the unfufpecting carelefnefs of a great Prelate in this particular has involved him in fo much trouble.------A trouble however to which we owe a beautiful picture of the moft virtuous mind and admirable abilities, triumphing over the impofture of others and the infirmities of his own great age. See the Bifhop of Winchefter's letter to Mr. Chevalier.*

"A letter

" A letter to James the Firſt §."

" An Epitaph [not bad] on Elizabeth Coun-
" teſs of Huntingdon ¶."

LUCIUS CARY,
LORD FALKLAND.

THERE never was a ſtronger inſtance
of what the magic of words and the art
of an Hiſtorian can effect, than in the character
of this Lord, who ſeems to have been a virtuous well-meaning Man with a moderate under-
ſtanding †, who got knocked on the head early
in the civil war, becauſe it boded ill: And yet
by the happy ſolemnity of my Lord Clarendon's
diction, Lord Falkland is the favorite perſonage

§ *Biogr. vol. 2. p. 1182.*
¶ *Memorials and characters of eminent and
worthy perſons, fol.* 1741 ; *in the appendix, p.* 15.
† *See his ſpeeches, which by no means ſhew great
parts.*

of

of that noble· work. We admire the pious
Æneas, who with all his unjuſt 'and uſurping
pretenſions, we are taught. to believe was the
ſent of Heaven ; but it is the amiable Pallas we
regret, though He was killed before He had performed any action of conſequence.

That Lord Falkland was a weak man, to
me appears indubitable. We are told He acted
with Hampden and the Patriots, till He grew
better informed what was ‡ Law. It is certain
that the ingenious Mr. Hume has ſhown that
both King James and King Charles acted upon
precedents of prerogative which they found eſtabliſhed.------Yet will this neither juſtify them nor
Lord Falkland. If it would, where ever Tyranny is eſtabliſhed by Law, it ought to be
ſacred and perpetual. Thoſe Patriots did not
attack King Charles ſo much for violation of
the Law, as to oblige him to ſubmit to the
amendment of *it :* And I muſt repeat, that it

---

‡ *It is evident from his ſpeech againſt the Judges
that this could not be entirely the caſe, for he there
aſſerts that thoſe Men had not only acted contrary to
ancient laws and cuſtoms, but even to ſome made in
that very reign.*

was great weaknefs to oppofe a Prince for breaking the Law, and yet fcruple to oppofe him when
He obftructed, the correction of it. My Lord
Falkland was a fincere Proteftant; would He
have taken up arms againft Henry the Eighth
for adding new nonfenfe to eftablifhed Popery,
and would He not have fought to obtain the
Reformation? Again :----When He abandoned
Hampden and that party, becaufe He miftrufted
the extent of their defigns, did it juftify his going over to the King? With what-----I will not
fay, Confcience.------But with what reafon could
He, who had been fo fenfible of grievances ‖,
lend his hand to reftore the authority from whence
thofe grievances flowed? Did the Ufurpation of
Cromwell prove that Laud had been a meek
Paftor? If Hampden and Pym were bad men
and ambitious, could not Lord Falkland have
done more fervice to the State by remaining with
them and checking their attempts and moderat-
ing their councils, than by offering his fword
and abilities to the King? His Lordfhip had felt
the tyranny; did not He know, that, if autho-

‖ *See his fpeech againft the Bifhops* ·

rized

rized by victory, neither the King's temper nor government were likely to become more gentle? Did He think that lofs of Liberty or lofs of Property are not Evils but when the Law of the Land allows them to be fo? Not to defcant too long; it is evident to me that this Lord had much debility of mind and a kind of fuperftitious fcruples, that might flow from an excellent heart, but by no means from a folid underftanding. His refufing to entertain fpies or to open letters, when Secretary of State, were the punctilios of the former, not of the latter; and his putting on a clean fhirt to be killed in, is no proof of fenfe either in his Lordfhip, or in the § Hiftorian, who thought it worth relating. Falkland's figning the declaration that He did not believe the King intended to make war on the Parliament, and at the fame time fubfcribing to levy twenty horfe for his Majefty's fervice, comes under a defcription, which, for the fake of the reft of his character, I am willing to call great infatuation. He wrote

"Poems."

§ *Whitlocke.*

"A Speech

"A Speech, on ill Counfellors about the
"King," 1640.

"A fpeech againft the Lord Keeper Finch
"and the Judges."

"A fpeech againft the Bifhops, February 9,
"1640."

"A draught of a fpeech concerning Epifco-
"pacy," found among his papers, printed at
Oxford, 1644.

"A difcourfe concerning Epifcopacy."

"A difcourfe of the infallibility of the Church
"of Rome." One George Holland, a popifh
prieft, replying to this, his Lordfhip publifhed
the following anfwer,

"A view of fome exceptions made againft
"the difcourfe of the infallibility of the Church

"A Letter to Mr. F. M." Printed at the
end of Mr. Charles Gataker's anfwer to five
captious queftions. Lond. 1673. quarto.

"A Letter

"A Letter to Dr. Beale, Master of St. John's
"College, Cambridge ¶."

He is said too to have affisted Chillingworth
in his book called, " The Religion of Protef-
" tants †."

HENRY CARY,

LORD FALKLAND,

DIED young, having given instances of
wit and parts. Being brought early into
the House of Commons, and a grave Senator
objecting to his youth, " and to his not looking
" as if he had fowed his wild oats," He replied
with great quicknefs, " Then I am come to the
" propereft place, where are fo many Geefe to
" pick them up." He wrote

¶ *Biogr. vol.* 2. *p.* 1182.
† *ib. p.* 1186.

" The

" The Marriage-night, a Comedy ;" abſurdly aſcribed by Antony Wood to the laſt Lord. His Son

ANTONY CARY,

LORD FALKLAND,

W^{ROTE}

" A prologue intended for the Old " Batchelor," but it ſeems to have had too little delicacy even for that play and that age.

Lord Lanſdown has inſcribed a copy of verſes to this Lord's Son, Lucius Henry, the fifth Lord Falkland, who ſerved in Spain.

THOMAS

THOMAS
LORD *FAIRFAX*,

T H E Parliamentary General. One can eafily believe his having been the Tool of Cromwell, when one fees by his own Memoirs how little idea He had of what he had been about. He left

" Short Memorials of Thomas Lord Fairfax,
" written by himfelf." Lond. 1699.

ARCHIBALD CAMPBELL,
MARQUIS of ARGYLE.

I T will not appear extraordinary, that this illuftrious blood which has produced fo many eminent Perfons, fhould have added to the Catalogue of Noble Authors from it's

own

own lift of Statefmen and Heroes. It is totally unneceſſary for me to enter into their characters, that 'taſk having been ſo fully performed by one § who wears the honour of their name, and who, it is no compliment to ſay, is one of the ableſt and moſt beautiful Writers of this Country.

In the Catalogue of the Harleian library, I find theſe ‖ pieces

"Marquis of Argyle his inſtructions to a "Son." 1661. It is obſervable that this Lord quarrelled both with his Father and his Son.

"His Defences againſt the Grand Indict-"ment of High-Treaſon." 1661.

§ *Vide the Lives of the Earls of Argyle, Biogr. Brit. vol. 2. pages* 1142, 1155.

‖ *vol.* 4. *p.* 817.

ARCHIBALD

ARCHIBALD CAMPBELL,

EARL of ARGYLE.

HAVING feen nothing of this Lord's compofition but his own Epitaph in verfe, written the night before his execution, he can fcarce with propriety be called an Author, no more than the Marquis of Montrofe, whom I have omitted, notwithftanding his well-known little elegy on King Charles. Yet Argyle's epitaph, though not very poetic, has energy enough to make one conclude that it was not his firft eſſay. At leaft there is an heroic fatisfaction of confcience expreſſed in it, worthy of the caufe in which he fell.

RICHARD MAITLAND,
EARL of ·LAUDERDALE,

Tranflated Virgil ; it was printed in two
volumes.. The manufcript was commu-
nicated to Mr. Dryden who adopted many of
the lines into his own tranflation.

COLIN LINDSAY,
EARL of BALCARRAS ;.

THE third Earl of that name, was of
the Privy Council and Treafury to James
the Second, to whom his loyalty was unfhaken,
as his character was unblemifhed. He was a
man of plain fenfe and fmall fortune, and left
a fmall volume of memoirs much efteemed,
intituled

" An account of the affairs of Scotland re-
" lating to the Revolution in 1688, as fent to
" the late King James the Second, when in

JOHN

JOHN DALRYMPLE,

VISCOUNT STAIR,

D'REW up " An Inftitute of the Law of " Scotland," which was publifhed in 1693, and was received with universal approbation ‡.

A N N E

COUNTESS of MORTON.

THERE goes under the name of this Lady a fmall book of Devotions, in which She afks God this meek queftion, " O " Lord, wilt Thou humble thyfelf to hunt " after a Flea?" But it appears by the preface that it was compofed by one M. G.

‡ *Biogr. Brit. p.* 2257.

IRISH PEERS.

GERALD FITZGERALD,

EARL of DESMOND;

THE fourth Earl of that line, was called the Poet, and for his ſkill in the mathematics was thought a Magician. This was about the year 1370‡.

GEORGE CALVERT,

LORD BALTIMORE,

WAS brought up under Sir Robert Cecil, and in 1619, attained the office of Secretary of State, which however He reſigned

‡ Lodge's Iriſh peerage, vol. I. p. 10.

con-

confcientioufly in 1624, on having embraced
the Roman Catholic religion. He remained
Privy Counfellor and was made a Baron. He
had the grant of Avalon, the firft Chriftian
fettlement in Newfoundland, whither He went
and defended it bravely againft the French; and
on it's being afterwards yielded to them, He obtained the grant of Maryland, of which his
family are ftill Proprietors.

We have this lift of his works ‡,

" Carmen funebre in Dom. Hen. Untonum ad
" Gallos bis legatum, ibique nuper fato functum."
1596. quarto. The Earl of Briftol wrote an
elegy on the fame occafion ‖ .

" Speeches in Parliament."

" Various Letters of State."

" The anfwer of Tom Telltroth."

" The practice of Princes and lamentation of
" the Kirk." 1642. quº·

" Something about Maryland." Not printed.

‡ *Biogr. Brit. vol.* 2. *p.* 1117. *Wood, vol.* 1.
p. 565.
‖ *See vol.* 1. *p.* 196, *of this work.* ROGER

ROGER BOYLE,

EARL of ORRERY,

A Man, who never made a bad figure, but
as an Author. As a. Soldier, his bravery
was diftinguifhed, his ftratagems remarkable ‡ :
As a Statefman, it is fufficient to fay that He
had the confidence of Cromwell: As a Man,
he was grateful and would have fupported the
Son of his Friend: Like Cicero and Richelieu
he could not be content without being a Poet.
The fenfible Author of a very curious life, of
this Lord in the Biographia feems to be as bad
a judge of poetry as his Lordfhip or Cicero,
when he fays that his. writings are never flat
and trivial.-----What does he think of an hundred fuch lines as thefe,

‡ *See his Life in the Biogr. Brit.*

"When

" When to the wars of Aquitaine I went,
" I made a friendſhip with the Earl of Kent ‖ ."

One might as foon find the fublime, or the modeſt, or the harmonious in this line,

" O Fortunatam natam Me Conſule Romam! "

Lord Orrery wrote

" The Iriſh Colours diſplayed ; in a reply of
" an Engliſh Proteſtant to a letter of an Iriſh
" Roman Catholic." Lond. 1662.

" An anſwer to a ſcandalous letter lately
" printed, and ſubſcribed by Peter Walſh, &c."
Dublin 1662, quº. and Lond.

" A poem on his Majeſty's happy reſtoration."
MS.

" A poem on the death of the celebrated Mr.
" Abraham Cowley." Lond. 1667. fol.

" The Hiſtory of Henry the Fifth, a tragedy."

‖ *The Black Prince, Act* V.

" Muſtapha,

" Muftapha, a tragedy."

" The Black Prince, a tragedy." •

" Tryphon, a tragedy."

" Partheniffa," a romance in three vols. fol. His Biographer feems to think that this performance is not read, becaufe it was never compleated; as if three volumes in folio would not content the moft heroic appetite that ever exifted!

" A Dream, a poem."

" The art of war." Lond. 1677. fol. Said to have been much ridiculed, but is applauded by the Biographia.

" Poems on the fafts and feftivals of the " Church." Printed, but never finifhed. I fhould act with regard to thefe, as I fhould about the Romance, not read them; not becaufe they were never finifhed, but becaufe they were ever begun. We are told his Lordfhip always wrote when He had a fit of the gout, which it feems was a very impotent Mufe.

The

The reft of his works were pofthumous,

" Mr. Antony, a comedy."

" Mr. Guzman, a comedy."

" Herod the Great, a tragedy."

" Altemira, a tragedy." All his dramatic pieces but Mr. Antony have been publifhed together in two volumes octavo. Lond. 1739.

" His State-letters." Lond. 1742. fol.

WENTWORTH DILLON,

EARL of ROSCOMMON,

ONE of the moft admired Writers in the reign of Charles the Second, but one of the moft carelefs too. His Effay on tranflated verfe, has great merit; in the reft of his poems

VOL. II.   E e   there

there are fcarce above four lines that are ftriking, as thefe,

"The Law appears with Maynard at their head,
" In legal murder None fo deeply read."

And thefe in the apparition of Tom Rofs to his
pupil the Duke of Monmouth,

" Like Samuel, at thy necromantic call,
" I rife to tell thee; God has left thee, Saul!"

His poems are printed together. in the firft
volume of the works of the Minor poets.

ROGER PALMER,

EARL of CASTLEMAIN,

AUTHOR of feveral pieces, but better
known by having been the Hufband of
the Duchefs of Cleveland, and by being fent
Embaffador from James the Second to the Pope;
who

who treated, him with as little ceremony as his
Wife had done. While her Grace was pro-
ducing Dukes for the State, the Earl was busied
in controversial divinity, and in defending the
religion of the Prince who was so gracious to
his Lady.

Of this Lord's composition I have found;

" An account of the present war between the
" Venetians and the Turks, with the state of
" Candie; in a letter to the King from Venice."
Lond. 1666; small twelves, with a print of
the Earl before it. In the Dedication he disco-
vers that the Turk is the Great Leviathan, and
that Renegades lose their talent for sea-affairs.

" A short and true account of the material
" passages in the late war between the English
" and Dutch. Written by the Right Honorable
" the Earl of Castlemain; and now published
by Thomas Price, Gent." In the Savoy, 1671.
The Editor, as wise as his Author, observes
that the Earl had visited Palestine, to which
He had a particular relation by his name *Palmer*
or *Pilgrim:* And he acquaints the World, that the
Earl's Great-Grand-father had three Sons born

for

for three Sundays fucceffively; and that another of his Anceftors with the fame Wife kept fixty open Chriftmas's in one houfe, without ever breaking up houfe.

" The Earl of Caftlemain's Manifefto." 1686. This is a defence of himfelf from being concerned in the Popifh plot, of which He was accufed by Turberville.

. " An apology in behalf of the Papifts."—This piece has not his name. It was anfwered by Loyd, Bifhop of St. Afaph, in 1667, and was re-printed with the anfwer in 1746.

" The Englifh Globe, being a ftabil and im-
" mobil one, performing what the ordinary
" Globes do, and much more. Invented and
" defcribed by the Right Honorable the Earl of
" Caftlemaine." 1679. thin quarto.

" The Compendium, or a fhort view of the
" trials in relation to the prefent plot, &c."

is afcribed to him, but I cannot affirm it to be
of

of his writing. I believe He wrote other things, but I have not met with them.

A fplendid book of his Embaſſy with cuts was publiſhed in folio.

ROBERT

VISCOUNT *MOLESWORTH*,

AUTHOR of that fenſible and free-fpirited Work,

" An account of Denmark."

And of theſe pieces,

" An addreſs to the Houſe of Commons for " the encouragement of agriculture."

" Tranflation of Hottoman's Franeo-Gallia."

And He is reported to have written other tracts in defence of Liberty, of his Country, of Mankind.

JAMES

JAMES HAMILTON,

EARL of ABERCORN,

W^{ROTE}

" Calculations and tables relating to
" the attractive virtue of Loadstones." 1729.

WILLIAM

VISCOUNT *GRIMSTON,*

I^S only mentioned here to vindicate him
from being an Author; having when a Boy
written a play called

" Love in a Hollow-tree," to be acted with his
school-fellows, the Duchess of Marlborough many
years

years afterwards procured a copy, and printed it, at a time that She had a difpute with him about the borough of St. Albans. Lord Grimfton buying up the impreffion, the Duchefs fent the copy to Holland to be re-printed. She made his Lordfhip ample reparation afterwards by printing her own Memoirs, not written in her Childhood.

F I N I S.

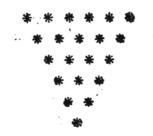

INDEX

TO THE

Second Volume.

NOBLE AUTHORS.

S U P P L E M E N T.

PEER-

INDEX

PEERESSES.

SCOTS AUTHORS.

Lord

INDEX.

IRISH PEERS.

Wentworth